Bedside Manna

Lionel Blue was born in the East End of London in 1930, the only son of a master tailor struggling in the Depression. He grew up surrounded by an extended family network of close relations and spent most of his days in his grandmother's kitchen where revolutionaries and the religious, intellectuals and poets talked and argued around him in Yiddish, White Russian, Hebrew and Cockney. To his surprise, he became a pillar of the religious establishment in charge of an Ecclesiastical Court, an editor of liturgy and a lecturer at a seminary. To the general public he is best known as a broadcaster, journalist, cook and author.

Bedside Manna

More Recipes for Body and Soul

Rabbi Lionel Blue

LONDON
VICTOR GOLLANCZ LTD
1992

First published in Great Britain 1991
by Victor Gollancz Ltd
14 Henrietta Street, London WC2E 8QJ
First published in Gollancz Paperbacks 1992

A catalogue record for this book
is available from the British Library

ISBN 0 575 05441 7

Printed and bound by
Cox & Wyman Ltd, Reading

Contents

Acknowledgements   9
Introduction   11
Conversions   14

APPETISERS
If I were a rich man   *Taramasalata*   16
Messing up marriages   *Green minty melon*   18
Uncle Joe   *Lemon kippers*   21
Blast from the past   *Mushrooms in cider vinegar*   23
Problems and turtles   *Spreading on beigels*   25
Helpful tips for Christmas, Chanukah or any
   time   *Stuffed pitta*   27
Chewing on Baroque   *Exotic sandwiches*   30
Creamy Brussels   *Herrings in cream*   32
Fit for a saint and a big black dog   *Stuffed sardines*   34

SOUPS
You-know-whose!   *Rich mushroom soup*   38
Life's simple pleasures   *Onion soup*   40
Living with God – How it is   *Party consommé*   42
A cookery correspondent   *Simple celery and lentil
   soup*   44
A washing-up meditation   *All-in-a-plate soup*   46
One man's best friend   *Pauline's quick tomato soup*   48
How you get into radio   *Georgina's lentil soup*   50
Religious temper   *Jewish-gentile penicillin – Kim's
   chicken soup*   52
My friend who fused the lights   *Cullen skink*   55
Patient survival   *Anglo-Chinese soup*   58

FISH
Cheer up and bake a pie   *Fish pie*   62
P . . . p . . . p . . .   *Granny's salmon fish cakes*   64
Waiting   *Omelette Hilda Lessways*   66

Waiter! Waiter!   *Granny's baked fish*   68
England, oh, my England   *Exotic fish fingers*   71
The elegant woman   *Trout Royale*   73
Practise as you preach   *Sister Lucy's haddock au
    gratin*   75
Fashion and fun   *Pasta with cauliflower sauce*   77
Templing and tombing   *Kim Holman's fish cakes*   79

MEAT
How does a cow emulate a hare *or* Going
    Dutch   *Theo's casserole*   82
Minding your own business   *Businesspeople's
    chicken*   84
Send an old friend a parcel of memories   *Cornish
    pasties*   86
Religion and the retail trade   *Honey meat loaf*   88
A stew is a stew is a stew . . .   *Carbonade*   90
A suitcase of memories in Berlin   *Polish beef olives*   92
Restaurant presence   *Father Robert's bobotie*   95

VEGETABLES AND SALADS
Revelling in autumn   *Comforting red cabbage*   98
On the yo-yo of life   *Cabbage noodles*   100
Food fit for a fast   *Simple savoury lentils*   102
Packaging holidays on a platter   *Sort of salad
    Niçoise*   104
Heaven   *Pennies from heaven*   106
Fashioning holiness   *Desperation beans*   108
What a tangled web we weave   *Exotic burghul salad*   110
A herbal remedy for healthy living   *Cauliflower salad* 112
Separate lives   *Frisian hunters' dish*   114
Moving on in life   *Party pie*   116

PUDDINGS
Tranquil hosts of a dream   *Crunchy, creamy apple
    pudding*   120
Breeteesh & Englisch   *Boodle's orange fool*   122
Old habits die hard   *Spiced Cox's apples*   126
Clerical epicures and gourmet ecumenists
    Tarte des demoiselles Tatin   128

My family of friends   *Sister Mary Camilleri's swift
    sweet*   130
Quelling quarrels with a carrot   *Quick lemon pud*   132
Cakes and counsel in teacup ministry   *Brown
    bread ice cream*   134
Singing nuns are now less frequent   *June's quick
    syllabub*   136
It wasn't jam!   *Mrs Carey's confection*   139

BAKING

How I learned to face up to my fear of
    hospices   *Sister Ann's Irish soda bread*   142
The Royal gentleman   *Richard's daily bread*   144
Have we got problems?   *Edith's South American
    cuca cake*   146
Old time office   *Banana bread*   148
French leave!   *Chocolate cake*   150
Poor tired shopper   *Dennis's Dundee cake*   152
Ma faces the music   *Richard's ginger biscuits*   155
The way we were   *Sister cook's daily oats*   157
Meditation on the New Year   *Anchoiade*   159
Pies for scousers   *Tom Trow's Cheese Pie*   161
In a crematorium canteen   *Molly's chocolate cake* 164

CURIOUS AND INTERESTING

Special   *Bandiera Italiana*   168
Birthday blues   *Quick Christmas pudding*   170
Horrible housework   *Slaphappy tuna snack*   172
What the past was like   *Bewildered pilchard pie*   174
'Saint Wulfstan is in the can'   *Cucumber soup*   177
Burnt offerings   *Barbecued red peppers
    Convenience coleslaw*   180
Wardwise   *Perfection*   182
Ordinary!   *Potato meat balls or in the Eastern part of
    Poland we call them 'Grapeshots'*   184
A lesson in RI   *Wild apricot jam*   186
Honesty   *Buckfast Abbey mince tarts*   188

Postscript   190
Index   191

Acknowledgements

I dedicate this book to the generous people who have shared their life's wisdom and kitchen lore with me – those who are named in the following pages, and those whose only memorial is their recipe.

My thanks to Pauline Whitehouse (now happily Mrs Knox-Crichton), who has checked through these recipes, and fed me for fifteen years. To Jim Cummings, who kept my head above a sea of paper, spilt cans, and olive oil bottles. To Kim Holman, who taught me to sail and to make a white sauce. Also to the innumerable clerics, rabbis, ministers, mystics, contemplatives and nuns who have become the sisters and brothers I never had.

And to you who read this book – I think of you as I munch and meditate, wondering who you are, and what you're up to.

Thank you, God bless, and bon appétit!

Introduction

Sometimes you wake up at night and want a book to read with a happy ending to help you through the depression that comes with the dead hours. Well, these days happy endings are even rarer in fiction than in life. But all is not lost, for recipes have in-built happy endings. I have fortified this collection with spirituality, and hope it will serve you when life has pulled the carpet from under you (as it has a habit of doing), or when you just want a giggle.

The recipes are non-neurotic. Many require no cooking – they are assemblage jobs, but none the less toothsome for that. Some are disaster-proof, and some you can cook up in a jiff and carry the result up to bed and consume while still only half awake. Provided you don't doubt yourself and show it, many will 'do' and do well for a dinner party. The best measures are your own cups and spoons. If you are reading a spiritual cookbook you will not want too many fluid ounces of this or milligrams of that. They make you tetchy!

In a later chapter I have said 'a stew is a stew is a stew' and this is very true. Whether you leave the bouquet garni in, and the garlic out, or add a slurp of cooking sherry and shake it all about, it's still a variation on the same theme. To few is it given to come up with a really original recipe. But though I rarely invent, I improvise and adjust because I live on the trot, and lack the time to organise myself or my store cupboard. Really recipes are like jokes. They change and can even improve in the telling. And just as no one knows who first told a joke, so it is with stews and casseroles, cakes and pâtés. I have tried to acknowledge those who inspired these dishes. Sometimes I just do not know, even after rummaging through the lumber room which is my mind and filing system. Sorry!

The recipes have been written on envelopes, on the backs of menus, in old diaries, and on visiting cards, and passed to me while washing up in retreat houses or sitting in the foyer of the BBC. Some will be familiar, or half familiar, to readers of the *Universe*, just as some you may have heard while taking your morning bath and listening to the BBC on your transistor. The nicest part of my life has been working for both organisations. By the way, you don't have to be a Catholic to enjoy the *Universe* – my mother and aunt fall upon each issue with gloating and glee, and they are Yiddisher girls. And you don't have to be officially pious to be caught up in a religious Thought or Pause. One important thing I have learned from the radio is that non-religious people are spiritual. They also know life isn't just things.

A word of explanation. It is commonly said 'we are what we eat'. But Jews, Moslems and many Eastern faiths also believe what they eat. Faith and food are so connected that theology and ritual dictate the recipes and the ingredients, and there are unexpected trip-wires for the unwary.

One of the Jewish ones, for example, is the prohibition against mixing milk with meat. You have to leave out one or the other, or use a substitute. Being an ingenious lot, Jews can produce many substitutes. I use 'chicken' and 'beef' stock cubes – good enough even for 'traditional' chicken soup and stews. I also use vegetarian chicken fat (used by Jews like dripping), and non-dairy milk, cheese and cream. The last are soya based, and their flavour has improved steadily over the years.

Another trip-wire is bacon. But smoked sausage, vegetarian 'smokey'-flavoured bits, and smoked beef, which is a bacon look-alike as well as a taste-alike, are available with a little searching.

With regard to the Jewish prohibition on shellfish, I substitute tuna, or flaked smoked fish. A friend uses parsnips for prawns in seafood sauce. She thinks they 'do'. I'm not so sure.

With Moslems of course there is the prohibition on alcohol. Grape juice is the best substitute.

The above accounts for some of the coy alternatives listed in these recipes. But few people ever cook a recipe exactly as it is written, and in cooking as in spirituality you have to find your own way home.

The same applies to using healthy ingredients. In the last few years our diet has come under close scrutiny. Some of the advice proffered is fad and fashion, much of it makes sense. Most of it I take on trust, as I have no special knowledge of digestion and its effect on my mind and soul – except that I am sure it has some. Fortunately, many acceptable substitutes for the less healthy parts of our diet are now easily obtainable. I use soya milk and cheese, or skimmed milk instead of my formerly favoured creamy bottles. I avoid the cholesterol of animal fats by eating vegetarian sausages and hamburgers. In health shops I buy egg substitute for cooking, or a dried egg powder that is calorie reduced and cholesterol-free for scrambled eggs and omelettes. The

'I was thinking, since food plays such a big part in our religion, we should change its name to Chewdaism.'

only thing I crave is strong central European cheese, the real stuff that comes from cows and goats not soya beans, that has a whiff of the farmyard which can knock you flat. Low-fat fromage frais and yoghurt can replace cream, and make a good base for salad dressings. I have also had to cut down on sugar, but aspartame sweetens my cereals nicely. It's worthwhile getting acquainted with your local health food shop. Drop in occasionally, as the range and variety of alternative foods is steadily increasing. Your curiosity and tastebuds will awaken together. Do use free range poultry, eggs and meat. Whether they taste better, I don't know, but they are better from a moral point of view.

A word on the spirituality! I have tried to express lightly but accurately what is not light to me. Not to be frivolous, but because life has a mirror-like quality. It reflects back the way you look at it. So it is more profitable to smile when you can. Surliness rarely pays.

This book can be taken in small doses and you need not start at the beginning. It may help you in a queue, in an underground station late at night, waiting for a bus or telephone call that doesn't come, or as an accompaniment to a box of chocs in bed.

Spirituality, food, work and sex are life's great preoccupations. This book combines the first two. The third requires separate treatment, and the last may be beyond my capacity.

Lionel Blue

A note about the illustrations

I am pleased and proud that these thoughts and recipes have been embellished by Nero. Now Nero is no Roman emperor but my old friend Harry Blacker, another grey haired Yiddisher boy like me. All the dramatis personae of Jewish life come under his kind, curious and critical gaze. Waiters, matriachs, and ministers of religion like me. You don't have to be Jewish to enjoy them – after all Jews are also human, only more so of course.

CONVERSIONS
Cups here and across the Atlantic
A British cup holds 10 fluid ounces, *or*
½ an Imperial pint (20 fluid ounces), *or* 300ml.
but
An American cup holds 8 fluid ounces, *or*
½ an American pint (16 fluid ounces), *or* 240ml.
An American cup holds just over 4oz (110g) of flour
and just under 8oz (225g) of sugar.
A metric cup holds 250ml, approximately the same
as the American cup.

Spoons
A level tablespoon holds about ½oz (10g) of flour or cocoa
or about 1oz (25g) of sugar, butter or rice.
American spoons are a little smaller than British ones.

> The recipes in this book generally serve 4 very hungry, or 6 moderately hungry people, but people's tastes and capacities are curious, so use your common sense.

Appetisers

I would like to say that appetisers are like the little encores that conclude concerts, but that is as silly as saying Oslo is the Cheltenham of the North, or Racine is the Shakespeare of France, or vice versa. Proust might get away with it, clerical cooks don't. And yet such trifles provide happier memories than the big dishes of Beethoven and Bartok they depend on.

The Greeks are sensible about it. A 'meze' is a meal of starters and appetisers, which lead to nothing except more of themselves. The best part of Russian cooking is the buffet of Piroshki, and in Sweden I would willingly leave the party while I am still sober and stuffed with sild and herring all marinated and wearing their heads.

I have had to restrain myself from making this section the centre-piece of the book; you can't live on nibbles alone. Life is serious, so the big stuff will follow. It will be good for you!

If I Were a Rich Man

Sometimes people ask me if Jews are rich – well, a few are, but most are lower or middle class, living in suburban semis. Many inhabit substandard housing in run-down inner cities. I know, because for years as their rabbi I wasn't explaining finer points of dogma to the faithful, just nagging the local council about leaking roofs on behalf of children with weak chests, and organising meals-on-wheels for old people whose lifetime of labour hadn't earned them much comfort.

Sometimes they burst into tears in my office, and I kept a kettle of boiling water on the go to make them lemon tea, to which they were partial. Even if I didn't have the lolly, I could listen. I also kept a bottle of rum, and a spoonful in a cup of lemon tea was luxury.

My oldies were a pious lot, and they called my cuppas 'the little resurrection', which is the nicest compliment ever paid to my cooking. They weren't envious of other people's good fortune, just wistful, like Topol singing 'If I Were a Rich Man'. We used to have sessions of wish-fulfilment, which always started off: 'Now, if you were a Rothschild, Rabbi, what would you do?' I would consider and say, 'I'd have smoked salmon every supper-time.' 'No,' they would say, 'you wouldn't, you would have chopped chicken livers with egg bread.'

There would be fierce differences of opinion, which would be resolved over another cuppa and a slice of bread and marge. Their Rothschild jokes were funny and kind. The Rothschilds were, of course, a Jewish family who'd made it and who inhabited another universe. But no one bore them a grudge for that.

Being poor doesn't mean that you are envious. After all, you never know how God is going to turn the wheel of fortune. Also, the Rothschilds had been generous with gifts and good deeds, giving large sums to charity, which is what God gave wealth for. Here is one of those stories, and I hope it cheers you up as it cheered me.

Two poor Jewish old ladies went to a posh synagogue in the West End. Looking down from the gallery they spied a beautifully dressed young boy. 'Who is that?' whispered one to the other. 'That's a Rothschild,' said the other, knowingly. 'My, my, so young and a Rothschild already!' replies her friend, in awe.

I couldn't feed my oldies smoked salmon, so I gave them taramasalata instead. They came from Poland and Russia and my taramasalata comes from Greece, but they relished it, and we decided it was a 'sort of' caviare. I sometimes think it's better, but I haven't had the opportunity to acquire the taste for the real stuff — like my oldies.

Taramasalata

8oz (225g) smoked cod's roe, from a jar or whole smoked cod's roe in its skin

6 slices of white bread de-crusted, soaked in water and squeezed out

4 tablespoons oil

2 tablespoons lemon juice

2 tablespoons chopped chives or finely chopped spring onions

2 tablespoons parsley

2 pinches sugar

white pepper to taste

2 cloves of garlic, crushed

● Put all the ingredients into a food processor and whizz until you have a stiff, pink cream. Turn into pots and chill.

● You can adjust the seasoning but be careful with salt — the cod's roe is very salty already.

● If you prefer the mixture thinner add some yoghurt or cream, but if you think it should be thicker, use more bread.

Messing Up Marriages

Though I am good at blessing babies I have never been too confident with weddings. Some of my colleagues have a flair for them, and nothing ever goes wrong.

It's not like that with me. In my time as a minister (and registrar for marriages) I've had to cope with so many crises that I have become as nervous as the bride and groom, and there have been times when all three of us were shaking during the ceremony like autumn leaves.

Such nervousness is dangerous in the Jewish ritual, because a lot of wine is involved. The wine, let me hasten to add, is symbolic, not sacramental, and has to be drunk twice by the groom and twice by the bride. But whatever its significance, it is red and it stains. A shaking goblet of wine in an unsteady hand is not the most comforting of sights for a nervous bride, whoever holds the goblet – the groom, the beadle or the rabbi.

Occasionally, the groom is the problem because he has enough 'nerves' for two. Somehow he has made his best man nervous as well, and between them they forget the ring. On more than one occasion I have had to take off my own signet ring and lend it to them. In their excitement they don't always give it back, and a stiff letter from me results in an apologetic reply from them. I can hardly run after their car, festooned as it is with ribbons, shouting, 'My ring, my ring! I want it back!'

I have, however, run after a wedding car waving a marriage certificate in my hands. These couples are so much in love that the recordings of registrars don't matter. But they do, they do, and one day they will be turning their house upside down to find out where they put that piece of paper.

In the Jewish ritual, at the end of the ceremony the groom breaks a wine-glass with his heel. There are many explanations for this. According to my teachers it is done to show that love is as difficult to create as a beautifully fashioned glass, but one careless word or action can smash it. It is a timely warning to the young couple.

On one occasion some of the guests played a dreadful trick on the groom. They substituted an unbreakable glass. The poor man pressed and pressed but nothing happened. The congregation began to titter nervously, and the bride was trembling in tears. Realising what had happened, I changed the glass, and gave several people a piece of my mind.

Another problem arises when, just before the ceremony starts, the couple – or one of them – decides they haven't made up their mind yet. I usually send them, without relatives, for a quiet cuppa on their own, and in the meantime try to keep the congregation entertained.

Having listed all these lamentable possibilities, I should like to

Something old – something blue!

assure you all that every couple I've officiated for has finally marched down the aisle, truly married to the music of Mendelssohn. Though how long my ritual 'glue' has lasted is another matter.

This melon appetiser will cool the emotions for a few hours, and the gin is good for the nerves.

Green Minty Melon

1 ripe melon
8oz (225g) seedless green
　grapes
4 kiwi fruit, thinly sliced

½ glass gin
handful of fresh mint leaves,
　chopped

● Peel and deseed the melon and cut it into grape-sized pieces, using one of those contraptions for making melon balls if you have one. Put these pieces with any juice you can salvage into a cut-glass bowl.

● Add the grapes, cut in half and deseeded where necessary, and the sliced kiwis.

● Sprinkle with the gin and chopped mint leaves and chill in the fridge. Serve with almond biscuits.

Uncle Joe

In Eastern Europe you never got hot news from the newspapers but from jokes whispered among friends. 'What's up?' 'Have you heard the latest?'

Well, a Stalinist party desperately looks for new members. If you recruit one you get fifty dollars reward. For two new members you get fifty dollars and permission to leave the party yourself. If you recruit three you get fifty dollars and a certificate that you were never a member of the party in the first place.

In its heyday, Stalinism worked rather like a religion. It had its sacred writings and heresies and it demanded complete commitment. No wonder then that some disillusioned party members now turn to religion. A market economy may satisfy your hungry body, but only belief can satisfy a hungry spirit.

Forty years ago I was having my first doubts about materialism, but I didn't find the changeover to religion easy. Three problems worried me, and my experience then may help others now.

The first was not what religion said, but how it said it, through stories, myths and parables, not scientific statements, and if you're modern this makes you want to give up. But Stalinism wasn't as scientific as it sounded, just as Bible stories aren't as artless as they seem.

Next problem. Did I have to believe the lot? Forty years ago I tried to and got religious indigestion. Take a text like 'I once was young and am now grown old but have never seen the righteous forsaken nor his seed begging bread.' Well the psalmist may not, but I have – many times. So I consider the statement, but I don't pray it.

And now bullseye! Are these stories fairy stories, comforting opium as Marx said? What's the evidence? I first looked for it in books and other people, but they either contradicted each other or had feet of clay. Then one morning I realised you have to become your own evidence by letting the God you worship refashion you. I should have guessed. Religious questions always boomerang back to you.

An old-time party member told me, in tears, that the revolution got hijacked because of personal ambition, greed and power. We tried to understand society to change it, he said, but we didn't start with ourselves. And this epitaph reminds me. Have you heard the latest?

Some hardliners pray for Stalin to return to earth. 'Come back, Comrade Stalin, and restore the party.' 'OK,' says Uncle Joe grudgingly, 'but I warn you – this time no more Mr Nice Guy.'

Now the cold war is over, hopefully recipes and tourism will replace propaganda and confrontation. East Europeans like smoked fish, but till now they have been denied our British best – bloaters and kippers. Bloaters are difficult to track down even here, but kippers are still humble and heavenly fare, and treated with imagination can give the same pleasure as smoked salmon.

Lemon Kippers

2 kippers, filleted
2 large lemons or bottled
   lemon juice
sunflower oil

1 dessertspoon green
   peppercorns – some of them
   crushed for flavour

●   Lay the kipper fillets in a shallow glass or china dish and just cover with the lemon juice. You can use bottled juice – make sure they are just covered and stay covered. If you float some oil on top this will put a film over the juice and prevent it evaporating. Throw into the lemon juice some crushed and some whole green peppercorns. Put the dish in the fridge overnight.

●   The next day take out the fillets and skin them (it comes off easily). The lemon juice will have 'cooked' them. Each kipper will provide two fillets. Serve drained with the peppercorns. The result is rich in taste and serves as a substitute for smoked salmon.

Blast From the Past

I decided to clear up the loft. There was a dusty box, filled not with old papers as I'd thought but with old records, a few 45s, but mostly scratched yet playable 78s.

A friend of mine had an old gramophone, a portable, with a little handle to wind it up. He had a friend who asked if he could come round and listen. He would bring along some of his precious thorn needles, he said, with a little machine to sharpen them. I suddenly remembered them. They were popular in the forties. Their sharpness lasted for one side only, and I was always being asked for emery paper to sharpen them.

The labels on the records were battered and faded, and none of us knew exactly what was going to come out of the soundbox. Solemnly we set the machine going and composed our faces for a serious message from the past. A high-pitched voice suddenly screamed out at us from the box: 'Why has the cow got four legs?' We looked at each other, while the voice continued: 'I don't know, and you don't know, and neither does the cow!' We burst into laughter. Being the oldest there, I knew who it must be. Only Cicely Courtneidge had that genial warm comedy which made you fall about with good humour.

On another 78, Sophie Tucker – the last of the red-hot mommas – sang of her own 'Yiddisher Momma', who never cared for fashion styles and who was also 'a shane Madonna, geshenkt fun Gott' – a beautiful Madonna sent from God! The words were 'schmaltz' but the sentiment was true, for such mommas existed, and I felt like crying as I wound the handle. The music still kept its magic.

When the evening was over and my friends had gone, I thought about those records before I said my prayers. To check my thoughts, I turned on the radio and listened to a pop programme. Yes, I was right, the old records seemed so innocent, even when they thought they were being naughty. There was no cruelty in the music. It must have been there in the people, of course, for after all it was the time of Hitler, but it wasn't respectable to reveal it.

This is an old-time recipe in my family, though it will be a new-time one to most people born and bred in Britain. It is good 'listening to' food. You need only bread, fingers, and kitchen roll.

Mushrooms in Cider Vinegar

1 lb (450g) button mushrooms, cleaned

1 teacup oil – sunflower and olive combined

¼ teacup cider vinegar

1 tablespoon dried sweet peppers

1 teaspoon black peppercorns

1 teaspoon salt

1 teaspoon mixed herbs including a bay leaf

4 cloves of garlic, chopped

1 teaspoon caster sugar

chopped fresh parsley

- In a saucepan simmer together for 5 minutes the oil, cider vinegar, dried sweet peppers, peppercorns, salt, mixed herbs, garlic and caster sugar.

- Add the button mushrooms and simmer for a further 5–6 minutes.

- Pour into a dish and leave the mushrooms to cool in their liquid. Chill.

- Scatter with chopped parsley and serve with a good quality cottage loaf to mop up the juices.

Problems and Turtles

I'm half on holiday, so I treat myself to a Yiddisher breakfast of beigels and kippers. And I listen in luxuriously to somone else's thought for his day on Radio 4. I get interested. He talks about some turtles with curious names. When washed in radioactive sludge, or effluent, they save the world. The effluent is Christianity, God, religion. The message fascinates me and the turtles intrigue me and I mull it over as I munch.

I tense up as I open my letters. It's interview time because of a TV series I'm involved in, set in the fifties. So far the critics have been a very decent lot, but I know what's going to happen. They'll start on spirituality and then my problems are bound to pop up. And, boy, did I have problems – straight, gay . . . you name it . . . falling for a fair gentile, depression, breakdown, overdose. My parents didn't know what hit them. Still, not guilty of dope, drugs, kids or mugging, and the last time I shoplifted, I was only six.

So how shall I handle it? Well, I can be flamboyant, but that's not me. I can avoid or evade my problems because some people prefer their ministers without them, smiling and blessing babies.

But that doesn't feel right either. My problems have turned into unexpected friends, and I can't cut them now. After all, I owe them whatever compassion I've got. They've made me friends too with fellow human beings I'd never have known otherwise: destitutes on London stations and people other people push around. Because of my own experience I feel for that Jewish boy who falls for the non-Jewish girl next door, though I couldn't change the rules to help him – or me. And God only happened when my problems got so big I couldn't carry them alone any longer and shouted 'Help'!

This is serious stuff and since I stopped smoking I must eat when I think. So I bite into my beigel and think about problems. They're not just a pain, they can be transformed into pleasure. I'm munching the evidence now. In the Middle Ages Jews weren't allowed to bake bread so they boiled their dough instead and the result is this beigel – a chewy delight. It's the same with this golden sludge called mayonnaise, which a cook concocted after a battle when he could only forage eggs and olive oil.

But more important than beigels, our problems can teach us pity. A few weeks ago a girl I knew tried to free a bird caught by its claw on a London bridge. No one wanted to know. Only two down-and-outs stopped and tried to entice it free with their sandwich.

So here's a suggestion! Invest in a beigel or sandwich today and sit on a park bench to eat it; while you're eating, meditate on your own sludge and effluent. Spiritually speaking, your problems might be the best present God ever gave you.

Mine didn't save the world, I admit — they weren't radioactive enough, but they saved me from a hard heart. And a gentleman doesn't disown his loyal, low, problematic friends, even when he's writing for such high-class company as you.

Now what do you spread on a beigel? Here are two suggestions.

Spreading on Beigels

MASHED KIPPERS AND EGGS

1lb (450g) boil-in-the-bag kipper fillets	juice of half a lemon
6oz (175g) soft margarine	1 clove of garlic, crushed
4 eggs, hardboiled	salt and 6 or 7 grinds of black pepper

● Boil the kippers in their bag. Throw away the skins but keep the juice. Mash them with their juice, the margarine, eggs, lemon juice and garlic. Season with pepper and taste for salt.

SMOKED MACKEREL AND BEANS

1 smoked mackerel fillet, skinned	1 dessertspoon horseradish sauce
1 large tin of butter beans, drained	1 tablespoon lemon juice
green part of 2–3 spring onions	1 teaspoon whisky, if you can bring yourself to spare it
	salt and pepper

● Process all the ingredients together until you have the texture you want, and season to taste. Add a little sunflower oil if it is too dry.

Helpful Tips for Christmas, Chanukah or Any Time

Here are some helpful tips for Christmas, Chanukah or any time.

If you're rummaging through the dirty laundry, looking for the least dirty shirt for the office party, wear it with a big bow tie because it hides the soiled neckline. If you've drunk too much at the said party, drink two pints of water to help against dehydration.

If money is tight this Christmas, what about some cheap treats. A thermos of hot chocolate by your bed, for instance, is a great comfort if you wake up worrying. And for outer warmth put some foil behind your radiators, then the heat gets reflected back on you.

If you feel alone, try single's clubs at churches and synagogues. But you are liable to bump into your ex.

You can sometimes get a free shampoo and set if you model for hairdressing students.

You may say, 'Rabbi Blue, Rabbi Blue, this is all very informative, but is it really spiritual enough, even for a religious cookery book?'

Funny you should ask that, because I once attended a conference entitled 'What is religion?' But I never learnt the answer because, like many middle-aged men, I was having prostate problems. As the experts trooped into the conference hall I frenziedly buttonholed them, whispering, 'Where's the washroom?' They waved their hands about vaguely. 'Find the porter, dear chap, he'll show you. Now I must get a good seat.' I was in agony until finally I located it in the basement. And while my colleagues considered the nature of religion in the conference hall above, I considered the same question from below.

Was religion what was going on in the conference hall above me, with its theories, debates, points of order and procedure? Possibly! They might be the manifestations of truth, they might also manifest prejudice and power. Are Christmas cards, Chanukah cards, turkeys, cranberries, candelabra, potato pancakes and presents religion? Yes, possibly! They might be the manifestations of care and kindness. They might also be silly spending on status objects.

So what is religion? Bible words from the synagogue service floated into my mind.

'Is it not sharing your food with the hungry and providing the homeless with shelter, clothing the naked when you meet them and not turning away your fellow flesh and blood?' And, I mentally added, 'Is it not showing a rabbi in agony the way to the washroom?'

'But, Rabbi Blue, Rabbi Blue, your hints about hangovers and dirty laundry are so earthy, so lacking in soul!'

Are they? I remember another saying, from the rabbis this time. 'A religious man looks after his own soul and other people's bodies. A hypocrite looks after his own body and other people's souls.'

'Tell me, Grandpa. Do gentiles also have Christmas parties?'

Stuffed Pitta

You can share your food with strangers easily by slitting pittas and stuffing them. They are Greek and Middle Eastern in origin but you can find packets of them now in lots of supermarkets. All you need to do is snip off the tops and they become containers you can consume. You won't have any washing-up as people can eat them in their hands, and unlike sandwiches the innards don't fall out.

What do you fill them with?

I like the nice Eastern Mediterranean combination of chopped spring onions, cucumber (peeled), white Feta cheese (cubed), cut-up tomatoes, chopped basil and a moistening (no more) of oil and lemon juice.

You can also use pitta like toasted crumpets. Pile tuna and Cheddar on top and lightly grill . . . but to go back to stuffing. Chick peas, chopped herbs and flaked smoked mackerel is a substantial filling for a main meal.

A non-Jewish friend – he calls himself 'bush Baptist' – assures me that avocado and crispy bacon is a knockout. I can't confirm or deny it. My Jewish-inspired rival filling is cold scrambled eggs (highly seasoned with pepper), mixed with cream cheese and cheap smoked salmon offcuts.

And finally, what about chopped chicken (free range or vegetarian) mixed with mayonnaise, chutney, and chopped ripe mango or apricots.

Yummy!

Chewing on Baroque

Quite a lot of people have written to me asking for advice on how to write a book. It's a bit like asking how long is a piece of string. I don't think any two writers use the same methods, and most writers don't know, even after the event, how they got it all together in the first place.

One writer I know, and a very successful one, can't write at home. He rents an office in which there is a minimum of furniture – one desk, one chair, a typewriter and paper – and stays there from ten to five with an hour off for lunch and fifteen minutes for elevenses. I, on the other hand, can write anywhere except in my office.

A park bench is fine, as is a crowded railway train, a café (the back of the menu) and a waiting-room in a hospital. The best time for me is about 6 a.m., when I am robed in a bathrobe of awful antiquity (Harrods 1936 cast-off) and about to drink a gallon of China tea. I like a bit of background noise, and keep Radio 3 on all the time. Baroque musical chewing-gum is soothing, and there seems to be lots of it.

The reasons why people write differ. Some write to earn a living, some write to express themselves, and some write just to find out what they are thinking. I often get down to writing as a way of re-entering the world. It takes me about an hour to cope with all the suffering you hear about on the news. That's why I get up early and pray a bit, write a bit and have sips of tea.

I think a good way to write is to buy a plastic bag, and every day put a fixed number of words into it (say 300 or 500). The trick is not to read back what you've written but put them straight in the bag. You can't judge your own writing just after you've written it – you always want to throw it away. When the bag is full, but only then, turn the contents out and see what you've got. Then your work really begins. With scissors and paste you now have to connect the bits together.

I often wonder how the writers of books in the Bible went about it. Some like Jeremiah were very upper class, and had a scribe – his was called Baruch, he tells us. But if Amos was a shepherd, how did he get it together? And what does it mean when it says at the top of Psalms 'To David, a hymn'? Did David write it, set it to music, edit it or just publish it?

When I'm writing I haven't got much time for cookery and I live very contentedly on sandwiches like these.

Exotic Sandwiches

CHICKEN LIVER AND ONION

8oz (225g) chicken livers, cleaned
½ onion, finely chopped
2oz (50g) butter or margarine
3 eggs

2 dessertspoons water
1 dessertspoon sherry
1 tablespoon chopped fresh parsley
salt and pepper
white bread

• Fry the onion in the butter or margarine until soft, not frizzled. Add the chicken livers and when they are cooked add the eggs beaten with the water and the sherry. Season with salt and pepper and mash with a fork as the eggs begin to set. It will firm up in the fridge if you want to eat it cold.

• Spread on white bread as open sandwiches and sprinkle with the parsley.

CURD CHEESE AND GHERKIN

8oz (225g) curd cheese
2 gherkins, chopped
1 small onion, finely chopped
½ sweet pepper, finely chopped

1 teaspoon paprika
1 tablespoon cream
salt
brown bread

• Mix all the ingredients together, season to taste and moisten with the cream until you have the texture you want.

• Spread on brown bread to make sandwiches.

Creamy Brussels

When the war ended I joined the other hopeful hitch-hikers lining the road to the Med. In 1946 there were no German cars, only stately English jalopies and tiny French ones with handcranks and horns. But sometimes a shark-shaped, American monster glided by, bearing Belgian numberplates. The driver clenched a cigar and beside him his blonde powdered her nose, heaving her bosom in time to our whistles. Once one stopped. The driver tossed me a cigar and his playmate breathed deeply in my direction. I was so overcome that on my next trip abroad I headed for Belgium.

It was the creamiest country I'd ever visited. The glossy chocolates oozed the stuff. And the culture was pretty creamy, too – the Rubens nudes were upholstered in such podgy pink and creamy flesh, I wanted to prod it. But what really threw me was the chips. I never thought you could gild that lily, but they did, adding a dollop of mayonnaise.

Many years later I returned to Belgium to address a conference. Arriving late and unprepared, I gave them my standard sermon against modern materialism, denouncing fridges, freezers and second cars, with side swipes at creamy chocolates. They gave it the standard applause. But next day a businessman jolted me badly. 'That was a very dangerous sermon, Rabbi Blue. Never run down fridges, freezers and cars, just pray that there'll be more of them for all of us. You don't remember the inflation, when people lost their savings, and the depression, when they saw their jobs disappear and they couldn't buy such things. That's when they turned nasty and passed the buck, and the concentration camps were born. When people are deprived and hurt, they hurt others. You as a Jew should know that.'

He was right, and I'll never preach such a silly sermon again. Here's my prayer and if he's still alive I hope he approves it.

'O Lord the source of our present prosperity, bless the Common Market in Brussels so that we may enjoy more of the same. Only help us not to clutch it, but share it and spread it around. And when it goes, help us not to whinge or pass the buck, but remember you are our God in bad times and good times alike, and the good life you taught us is greater than good living. Amen!'

Nowadays the new Common Market sky-scrapers tower over the provincial market town that once was Brussels. It hasn't got the culture of Rome or even nearby Bruges. And its war memorials are not on the same scale as the Arc de Triomphe or the Siegestor in Berlin. But it's still the best place to eat in Europe, and its cuisine bourgeoise beyond comparison.

Romantics sometimes sneer at its sensible earthiness, which is why it's the safest place to be Europe's capital. In fact I can only think of one better – polite and placid Luxembourg, where no university disturbs the digestion and you get even more mayonnaise on your chips.

Herrings and cream are good Belgian staples. In this recipe they marry nicely.

Herrings in Cream

1 large bottle of pickled herrings
¼ pint (150ml) double cream or yoghurt
1 tablespoon lemon juice
2 tablespoons mayonnaise
1 tinned red pimento, finely chopped
2 tablespoons chopped chives
2 tablespoons chopped fresh parsley
1 dessert apple, peeled, cored and finely chopped
½ stick of celery, finely chopped
1 level teaspoon sugar
salt and a pinch of white pepper

● Drain the herrings well, removing any pickling spices, and cut off their tails.

● Mix together the cream, lemon juice and mayonnaise. Add the pimento, chives, parsley, apple and celery. Now season with the sugar, salt to taste and a pinch of white pepper.

● Pour the cream mixture over the herrings in a serving dish and let them marinate for several hours in the fridge.

● This is very good with rye bread.

Fit for a Saint and a Big Black Dog

In Judaism the word saint is usually reserved for God, not individuals, so I only got introduced to saints when studying history, and their lives thrilled me. I liked the one who beseeched God because he was too good looking, and God fitted him with a dog's head. Regretfully, that wasn't my problem and little Thérèse and her cry for truth alone was more relevant.

So I was interested when a friend rang me with the latest talk on possible candidates for canonisation. He mentioned Pope John XXIII and Pius XII, alone or in tandem, Isabella of Spain, the Austrian Franz Jagerstätter, our own Cardinal Newman, and the usual nuns. 'And miracles are no longer necessary,' he sighed, being of the old school.

I clucked sympathetically, but hung up because it wasn't really my problem. I'd enough of my own, the most pressing of which was a black dog, too old like me, abandoned without a collar, on my doorstep.

Now I can't keep a dog, I'm away too much. So I decided to leave it some food well away from the house. But that's when the saints come marching in to this story, for I suddenly remembered Franz Jagerstätter whom my friend had mentioned — the unpolitical Austrian worker who got beheaded because he wouldn't join the German army, not even the non-combatant corps, despite the pleading of his priest, his bishop and his family. It didn't feel right, and like Luther he could do no other.

And I could do no other either. You can't turn out a fellow creature into a night not fit for a dog. You can only calculate with your conscience so far, and then comes the crunch, whether it's Hitler or a dog on your doorstep. Now religious people are specialists in that crunch, even though they've no special aptitude for politics. We are only amateurs in a highly professional business who get criticised because we confuse goodness with power and resolutions with reality.

But that crunch is beyond politics; it's the bottom line below which you begin to lose your soul and God is in it. Franz Jagerstätter recognised it in his life, and so should you in yours because it affects your fate not just in this life but in whatever life lies beyond it.

But back to Bonzo! He slept that night by the living-room radiator, while I worried about what to do with him. I fell asleep, deciding only to call him Jake after Jagerstätter, for that's whom he owed his warm bed to. It's no miracle, I admit, but perhaps Jake can still help Jagerstätter's cause. After all, one good turn deserves another and we need reminding that not everything in life is negotiable.

Now these nut-stuffed sardines are appropriate, because they remind me of home; Jake also liked fish, because on our first night together we shared a grilled boned mackerel.

Stuffed Sardines

1lb (450g) fresh sardines
1 tablespoon chopped nuts, such as cashews, pine nuts or almonds
2 tablespoons chopped fresh parsley
2 tablespoons brown breadcrumbs

1 clove of garlic, crushed
1 heaped tablespoon of sultanas or currants
3 tablespoons olive oil
3 tablespoons lemon juice
salt and pepper

- Slit the sardines down their tummies and clean.

- Mix the chopped nuts with the parsley and breadcrumbs, the garlic and the sultanas or currants. Season the mixture with salt and pepper and put a dollop of the stuffing inside each sardine.

- Lay the sardines in a baking dish and drizzle over the olive oil and lemon juice. Bake for about 15 minutes at Gas 5/375°F/190°C.

- Eat hot with French bread.

Soups

'Who for such dainties would not stoop,
Soup of the evening, beautiful soup.'

Soup is not just beautiful to eat or drink, it is also beautiful to make. When life gets too much for me I wander down to the kitchen and start by softening an onion . . . Then there is the discovery of unsuspected treasures in the vegetable basket, and the further reaches of the refrigerator. Soup-making can transform lumps of turnip, and lumps of anger. Provided you stir your pot with attention and affection, and with no bad vibes, and you taste frequently, little can go wrong. The result will sometimes be gourmet, usually only pleasant peasant, but iced in a summer garden, or hot on a winter evening, it is just right. Recycling waste has become a moral imperative, and soup-making is the most sensible expression of it. Stir, stir, it's good for stress!

You-Know-Whose!

I took over our household cooking three years ago because my mother and aunt couldn't handle hot oil. Straightaway I had to quell a mutiny – 'Chuck the stove, Lionel,' said my mother. 'Let's get a microwave and eat Chilli con Carne straight from the foil packets – then there won't be any washing-up.'

To shame her I decided to cook some real food. I peeled and stewed organic tomatoes. I added vegetables, then sieved them out. I infused fresh herbs. I thickened, emulsified and tested. The result was red, reassuring and familiar. 'Why,' said my mother admiringly, 'it's tomato soup, just like you-know-whose. I always preferred that brand.' I snatched her ladle, and tasted again. 'It *is* familiar – *over* familiar! . . . When two extra guests turn up, I add a can of you-know-whose, and nobody will notice the difference.'

Now, after doing dinners for three years, I'm no longer romantic but realistic. I whoop round the supermarket in search of convenience offers. I can't do without them, but I can't do with them as they are, either. They're too bland and a cook has his pride.

I've solved the problem by personalising my packets. I slurp cheap sherry into mushroom soup mix and puréed pimentos into tomato ditto. I hot up baked beans with chilli, and lift frozen strawberries with a grind of pepper. OK, you prefer cream not pepper – sorry, mate, it's my cooking!

I brood over this while stirring soup. It's boring work, so I twiddle my kitchen transistor, and tune into a breezy religious broadcast from a commercial station. It's pious stuff, creamy and easy to swallow. In fact, packaged religion is as bland as packaged food. Because it has to be right for everybody it's never quite right for anybody. It's like those overblown good wishes on Chanukah and Christmas cards, under-neath fat robins, candelabra and carousing cardinals. Unless you scrawl in some real wishes of your own, they're empty.

Suddenly, I hit on the answer to a question that's been worrying me.

People ask me sometimes why religion's gone flat on them, expired for lack of oxygen. Well, have you ever personalised the package you received at Sunday school? Have you stirred your own truth into the truths they taught you and flavoured them with your own life experience? It isn't enough to eat potato pancakes and light Chanukah candles – *you* have to be enlightened, too. It isn't enough to send pictures of a baby born in Bethlehem – something has to be born in you.

I'm excited and on the edge of a profound thought when my mother sings out, 'The soup's boiling over!' In the recriminations that follow I forget what I was thinking.

'I told you to get a microwave,' grumbles my mother. 'Lionel, look at all that washing-up!'

Rich Mushroom Soup

8oz (225g) white button
mushrooms, sliced
2 tablespoons butter or
margarine
1 large tin cream of mushroom
soup
1 large tin cream of onion or
chicken soup

½ pint (300ml) single cream
(or non-dairy substitute)
1 tablespoon dry sherry
grated nutmeg
salt and pepper
5 tablespoons chopped chives
or the green of spring onions

● Stew the sliced mushrooms in the butter for 3–4 mintues.

● Add the tin of mushroom soup, the tin of onion (or chicken) soup, the single cream, dry sherry and grated nutmeg to your taste. Simmer very gently for 10 minutes.

● Season with salt and pepper and stir in the chopped chives.

Life's Simple Pleasures

A friend of mine wrote to me from Dublin about the rise of technology and the decline of simple pleasures. He wasn't against labour-saving devices but he pointed out something which startled me.

In the old days, before people used washing-machines or launderettes, they used to scrub their smalls on tin or glass boards (you never see them now). It wasn't wonderful work, he said, but what was wonderful was that they sang as they scrubbed. He had never heard anyone croon over a washing-machine unless they were drunk, which didn't count. I began to think of the simple pleasures I have known that haven't survived technology . . .

After Christmas this year I saw some children throwing away their old Christmas cards. I looked horrified, and they asked me if anything was the matter. Yes, I said, and told them to bring me scissors, paste and an unused drawing-book. We sat down and cut away and made something magical out of the cards. There were silver stars and gilt greetings and reindeer that had strayed from Lapland to Bethlehem. One little girl told me that she would keep this scrapbook for ever. Promises, promises!

When our house was blown up in the Blitz, the only bits of the past I saved were a bear with one eye and two scrapbooks − all my own work, though a kindly uncle used to manage the scissors for me.

If scrapbooks are too wayward and unprogrammed for you, then the next best thing is a cut-out book of one of Pollock's toy theatres. Years ago I bought one and made a Victorian stage, showing the pantomime of Aladdin. Pollock's give you the character cut-outs and the original text, too, so you really are recreating a piece of history. Pollock's, by the way, is near Goodge Street station in London. There was a Mr Pollock once who had a toyshop long ago and left it as a toy museum for children. I used to visit it to try out the toys but now I go to listen to the music-boxes. They restore my balance after too many bombs explode in the news.

Making soup is a simple, soothing pleasure. There is little to go wrong, and it is always superior to the sachets, packages and tins of the prepared stuff, though they are good to add to your creation.

Onion Soup

4 large onions, sliced
2 cloves of garlic, sliced
2 tablespoons oil
2oz (50g) butter or margarine
½ teaspoon sugar
2 pints (1.2 litres) stock
6fl oz (200ml) vermouth or
   white wine

a large sprig of rosemary
salt and pepper

Garnish
slices of French bread
grated cheese

● Soften the onions and garlic slowly in the oil (I use olive) and butter. As they cook, sprinkle them with the sugar; this will caramelise them, but do not let them go dark brown, just a pleasant beige.

● Add the stock (you can use cubes), the vermouth or the remains of a bottle of white wine, and the sprig of rosemary. Season to taste and simmer away for 30 minutes. Remove the rosemary at the end.

● Some people float slices of French bread on top, covered with cheese, the whole dish finished off under a grill to melt the cheese. I prefer to have a separate bowl of grated Lancashire cheese and let everyone help themselves – though it's delicious without cheese, too.

● Instead of stock, I often use 2-pint packages of French onion soup mixed with water. Purists, I know, would not approve, but I am not a perfectionist – life is too complicated for such capers. Yes, there is a commandment to be perfect in the Bible. You can find it in the nineteenth chapter of Leviticus. I believe the Hebrew 'perfect' means either 'innocent' or 'whole, complete'. If you keep to my translation, you won't be such a pain in the neck to yourself or others.

If you prefer your onion soup thick, you can amalgamate 1 heaped tablespoon of plain flour with the onions, fry and then mix slowly with the stock. If you are beyond shame, like me when I'm rushed, thicken with onion gravy granules towards the end. No one has ever noticed the difference.

Another tip. Experiment with two or three cracked cardamom seeds, before you boil up.

Living with God – How It Is

Sometimes a radio station rings me up to ask me to give some talks.
'Look,' they say, 'prepare five scripts in advance and we'll arrange a
time for you to come in and record them all together. It will save an
awful lot of trouble.' But the trouble is, all religious talks, radio ones
too, involve God, and with me God doesn't work that way. It takes two
to tango, whether it's in a dance hall or a prayer hall.

You only learn about the way God works in you from experience.
Scriptures and service books tell you how he works with other people.
They're helpful but the proof of the pudding is in the eating.

Anyway, here's what I've learned. God and I met forty years ago
exactly. Either I discovered him or he discovered me. I don't know

'Dear God, you help
strangers, so why not
help me?'

which. We've had our ups and downs, and sometimes I've wanted to
walk out on him, but we've stuck together, so it's more like a marriage
than an affaire.

One thing I do know from experience is that he doesn't come to help
me in advance. He'll give me my daily bread, but not my next month's
supply. He won't tell me what the cosmos is about, he just gives me
that bit of extra courage as I need it. He'll help me to write tomorrow's
talk, but he won't help me to write five in advance. Yes, it's awkward
and not so efficient, but that's what he's like, and I've learned to live
with it and put up with it.

I also find I can't always meet him when and how I like. It's when
and how *he* likes, too. I go to a service, I screw up my eyes to
concentrate, I say all the right things and join in the responses, and the

result is – well – nix! It's like talking to thin air. There's nobody in!

And then that evening when I go to a party, I find he's come along too, though he wasn't invited. 'Invite that shy girl over there to dance, Lionel,' he says quietly. 'You'd be doing me a favour.' Well, he's done me a lot of favours, so I put down my glass and my sandwich, and wander over, all casual like, and say, 'Would you like to dance? I'm not very good at it, I'm afraid, but I'd be so grateful, etc., etc.' I know from the relief in the girl's eyes that he was spot on, and I feel warm and comfy inside, as I always do when we're both on the same wavelength.

Later on in the kitchen, when I'm on my own, tasting the remains and helping my hosts with the washing-up, I know he's there beside me, and there's nothing I need to say.

Now, what was in that girl's glass at the party? If I was doing the catering, not what you might think – not cocktails or gin but consommé.

Party Consommé

For rather grand consommé, you will need for every three people:	1 tablespoon sherry 3 teaspoons Danish lumpfish 'caviar' (either red gold or black) 3 tablespoons sour cream lemon slices
1 tin of condensed consommé (beef, chicken or vegetarian) 1 small, ripe avocado, peeled, stoned and diced	

● Empty the consommé into a bowl, and leave it to jell in the fridge overnight. Stir in the avocado and sherry.

● Divide between three glasses. Chill again and before serving add 'caviar' on top of the jellied consommé and a blob of sour cream on top of that. Curl a lemon slice on top. Make sure it is consumed straight-away, otherwise it will melt. Serve with a small glass of iced vodka or Dutch geneva if you have it. If you haven't, don't fret!

● To make a vegetarian consommé, you will need to use agar-agar to jell the soup (non-vegetarian consommé already contains gelatine). You can get it in health shops. Follow instructions on packet.

A Cookery Correspondent

Many years ago, I became cookery correspondent for the Catholic paper, the *Universe*. It began as a joke and has gone on now for fifteen years. Each week the Christian paper plops through my letterbox, just as they deliver a Jewish weekly with the same format.

My elderly mother and aunt grab both before I can get at them. They sit in facing armchairs, cannibalising them and pulling their pages apart, shouting out juicy extracts and passing pages to each other. Then they roughly reassemble the remains, and virtuously return them to me.

I settle down for a serious read, turn a page, and wonder with astonishment what on earth Sister Gloxinia is doing in the kosher column — and surely old Rabbi so-and-so isn't retiring to Lourdes. I used to go red with rage. Now I just giggle and enjoy.

Radio, TV and newspapers have broken down our ghetto walls and mixed us all together willy-nilly. One nice result is that we've got to know each other as friends and neighbours, which didn't happen that often in the old days, when Jews lived on one side of the street and Christians on the other, and we never got beyond polite 'Good morning's. It was the same with Protestants and Catholics.

But this closer acquaintance also can cause real problems. Take services at inter-faith conferences. Some join in their neighbour's prayers and sound insincere. Some leave out the words that don't fit their own religion and the result is pious confetti. Some say nothing and feel left out. That's why people of different faiths can often only sit together, holding hands, and sharing prayers in silence.

I've found this silent prayer — which started off as a service sub-stitute — more and more attractive, and use it even when I'm on my own. It's such a simple, direct way to God. You don't need props like prayer books, and you can practise it anywhere, on a park bench, in a queue at a check-out or on an underground platform.

How does it work? Well, for me silence is like layers.

First, I feel twitchy and self-conscious. Then I relax and listen to a bird singing or a distant train. Then suds of self-pity, spiked with temper, and sexy bits float through my mind. I get embarrassed and want to turn on the TV. But as the fluff settles, a shaft of sunlight gleams through. If you've got a fertile religious imagination, like me, the sunlight seems to speak, and you can have a conversation with it. If you're a more sober type, well, just say you've struck some source of joy and kindness you never thought you had in you.

But please don't take any of this on trust. Take ten minutes off – settle down comfortably and try it yourself. In the silence you may be surprised by that same sunlight, shining in you.

A kitchen can serve as a hermitage if you are left alone in it, and your cooking is not of the twitchy type. Little can go wrong with this simple soup, and you can meditate as you stir. Green lentils are superior to the pink ones – they don't crumble. Use them with good quality olive oil.

Simple Celery and Lentil Soup

1 large onion, chopped	6oz (175g) green lentils
2 cloves of garlic, finely chopped	1½ pints (850ml) water or light stock
2 tablespoons decent olive oil	salt and freshly ground black pepper
1 head of celery, cleaned	

● Soften the chopped onion and garlic in the oil (do not allow to brown). Roughly chop the outer stems of the celery and add, along with the lentils. Turn in the oil, then add the water or stock. Simmer for 30–40 minutes.

● Sieve (a mouli is the best instrument for this). Return to the saucepan and season with salt and black pepper. Add the inner stems of the celery, finely chopped, and allow to simmer until the celery is cooked but crunchy.

● If you like croûtons they'd be good with this.

● You can of course make any soup thick by using less liquid or stock; the result in this recipe is a lovely thick lentil stew. Ladle into bowls and put olive oil, red wine vinegar and chopped raw red onions on the table, for each diner to stir into her or his bowl. The wine vinegar is essential. No, it can't be malt!

A Washing-up Meditation

Washing up can be a delightful occupation, provided you set about it with the right attitudes and in the right conditions. Now these vary from person to person, and the following are my own.

First, I don't want to do it when other people are around. It's a mucky business and I spill things – water slops over the sink and cooked cabbage falls on the floor. I don't mind mopping up or picking up, so long as no one is going to mutter tut-tut.

Second, I need a voluminous old bath robe to do it in. Most aprons are too skimpy to suit my style and easily get waterlogged. Never, never, tell yourself you'll be extra careful and wash up in your best clothes uncovered. As my religious teacher used to say, 'Never trust in yourself till the day of your death.' The way to the dry cleaners is paved with good intentions.

Next, if nobody is around feel free to nosh. It's amazing what delicacies people leave on their plates, and provided your friends are a hygienic and healthy lot it seems a pity to waste them. Why should Fido or Pussy scoff the lot. Humans have rights, too. Here's to Human Lib. (You can make yourself a cook's cocktail by mixing the dregs of bottles. The colour, the taste, the 'nose' can be truly remarkable.)

Though I don't want other people around in person, I do want the radio. I like to sing as I swill. Pop, opera or oratorio, I don't mind which. It's nice to have some big band or choir to singalong with. It also covers the noise of any cup that cracks, or glass that splinters, so it's strategic.

For those who don't like cleaning pots and pans, which is, I admit, the part I like least, here is an all-in-one supper dish. It was given to me by my friend Dr Wendy Greengross, whom you may know because of her work for Cheshire Homes, or as media agony aunt.

The quantities here satisfy eight diners, and especially the cook because it's easy.

All-In-A-Plate-Soup

Serves 8

4 medium onions, chopped
2 tablespoons oil
4 pints (2.4 litres) water
6 carrots, sliced
2 parsnips, sliced
½ cup pearl barley
1 14oz (380g) tin of tomatoes *or* 1lb (450g) cooking tomatoes
1lb (450g) minced meat

1 egg, beaten
3 slices white bread, crumbed
8 medium potatoes, peeled and halved
Optional Extras:
shredded cabbage, celery, sweet corn, peas or beans (fresh or frozen)
salt and pepper

● Fry the onion in 1 tablespoon of the oil.

● Boil the water in a large saucepan, and add half the fried onion, three carrots, one parsnip, the pearl barley and the tomatoes. Simmer gently for 1 hour.

● Mix together the meat, remaining fried onion, well-beaten egg and breadcrumbs. Roll into small balls and fry for a few minutes in the remaining tablespoon of oil.

● Add the meatballs to the soup, with the remaining sliced carrots and parsnip, and the potato halves. Simmer for 20 minutes. Add salt and pepper, take off the heat and allow to stand for 20 minutes.

● Add all other vegetables, bring to boil and simmer for 10 minutes. Serve in soup plates with French bread.

One Man's Best Friend

I have always liked autumn. I used to chase my dog, Re'ach, who hunted sticks through London's parks and heaths. Re'ach regarded all sticks as hers by right, and when she saw two stockbroker types by a pond, pointing to distant spires with their brollies, she thought they were playing 'sticks' and there were words and woofs on both sides. Re'ach got pushed into the pond, but she splashed their spats as she fell, so the score was even. I witnessed this from behind a bush where I was hiding, pretending not to know either dog or stick.

I also like autumn because of the harvest festivals and services. Priests and pastors peer from pulpits, draped in greenery like timid Tarzans, and you catch sight of choir ladies smiling between clusters of root vegetables and giant marrows.

Some ministers are not content with blessing apples and broccoli or such, but venture from the vegetable into the animal world. Now, such things were all right for St Francis, who got on with the wolf of Gubbio, but I suggest you practise hallowing hamsters and blessing budgies before you try to missionise big game. I say this with feeling, because I once took Re'ach to an animal blessing just after I first bought her. It was a dreadful mistake.

She saw a hamster – her first – and she couldn't believe it. She raved as if it was a rat, and both of us were ejected. Re'ach regarded this as a triumph, but I decided never to bless anything larger than a budgie. I didn't have it in me.

Autumn is also a time for marshmallow-toasting over a coal fire, and warming meals eaten in comfort, with the curtains drawn at dusk.

This is an undemanding, cosy recipe, appreciated by man and beast (see above), given to me by my friend Pauline. It makes a change from you-know-whose!

Pauline's Quick Tomato Soup

1 onion, chopped
1 or 2 cloves of garlic, finely
  chopped
1½ tablespoons sunflower
  oil
2 14-oz (380g) tins of chopped
  tomatoes

1 light stock cube diluted in ½
  pint (300ml) hot water
basil
juice and zest of half an orange
salt and pepper
1 teaspoon sugar
yoghurt to serve

● Fry the onion and garlic in the oil till brown. Add the tomatoes and stock, the basil (which is particularly good, though you can use any herbs you like) and orange juice and zest to taste. Season with salt, pepper and sugar.

● Simmer for 20 minutes, and then liquidise with a processor or mouli. Serve with a blob of yoghurt in each helping.

How You Get Into Radio

People sometimes ask me how I got into radio. Well, I didn't plot it or even intend it. Like most important things in life, it happened by accident.

They were doing a sort of 'Down Your Way' programme in a synagogue whose minister I had been many years before. I was working at that time in Brussels and was hurriedly summoned back. Now in Brussels I had just gone to a wedding banquet, and I had to rush away from it with a wine glass in my hand to get the night boat train to London. I was feeling queasy before I even got on the boat. The weather was rough, the saloon was blue with smoke, and I was as sick as a dog.

I arrived in London feeling weak and wan, and took a taxi to my old synagogue to be interviewed. I was so weak and wan, in fact, that I couldn't compose polite and politic answers. I was just able to say the first thoughts that came to mind – which, I freely admit, were not the wisest or most prudent.

I was asked to elaborate on one and, to my horror, I heard myself coming out with an unsuitable anecdote told me by the steward on board. 'Well,' I said to myself, 'Lionel, old boy, you've certainly fluffed it this time.' This didn't worry me, because I had no radio ambitions, and I never thought they would ask me again.

But, to my surprise, they did! By accident I had stumbled on one of the truths of radio religion. You don't have to be the wisest, wittiest or profoundest of people, but you do have to be yourself. Looking at the greats on TV or listening to them on radio, that is something they all have in common – they are the same people on the screen as off.

One of the nice things about being a journalist, whether on a paper or over the radio, is that people send you letters which tell you a lot about their lives and their recipes.

Here's one from Georgina Fowler, from Greece. It's a comfortable and delicious peasant dish – which you can eat as a stew or as a soup – and I had never combined lentils with milk before. I used the brown sort not the red ones, but I think the recipe works with all types. It is also quick, like French onion soup, and useful for when you are extending your home, your table, your bedding and the larder to welcome suddenly descending children and friends – I like recipes like that.

Georgina's Lentil Soup

1lb (450g) brown lentils, well washed
3fl oz (75ml) olive oil
½ pint (300ml) milk

1 level teaspoon cumin
salt and freshly ground pepper
optional: stock, 1 lump of best butter

- Cook the lentils in water until soft.

- Drain and return to the pan with the oil and milk; stir like mad. Season with the cumin, salt and pepper.

- At this point you can turn the dish into a soup by adding stock to the consistency that suits you. A walnut-sized lump of butter goes well, enriching flavour and texture if the olive oil is not fruity enough.

Religious Temper

I'm a pardon-me-for-living person, not a short-fuse person. And when I lose my temper, religion is responsible. A while ago I was asked to preach at a service. 'Sorry,' I said, 'I have to prepare a radio talk.' 'But that's only light entertainment. Think up some silly joke.' I seethed because a 'simple' radio talk needs more thought than any sermon. And that's not because more people listen than in all the congregations I've ever preached to added together.

It's because if I say something silly on a pulpit it sounds serious, but if I say the same thing between two pop records it sounds too slight, unless I'm very exact. Also, in a half-hour sermon, you and your message should bump into each other along the way, but in three minutes every word counts. You haven't time for fuss.

And, more important, for me entertainment isn't light, it's a social service. You don't have to live in the Third World to be deprived. Stress and insecurity are our counterpart to its hunger and thirst. A friend of mine who slept on the pavements of Bombay remarked on how unhappy people looked when he returned to London. They had everything, but enjoyed nothing.

Entertainment is holy, too. I wander around hospital wards. Life's unfair, but there's nothing you can do about that, except that it has a strange mirror-like quality, which reflects back the way you look at it. If you look at life with hate, it is hateful. If you can smile into it, the whole world smiles with you. There's a strange story in the Talmud about Rabbi Baruka, who once bumped into the prophet Elijah in a crowded shopping centre. 'Which people here will have eternal life?' he asked him, and Elijah pointed to two buskers. Rabbi Baruka approached them to find out what was so special about them. 'When a fight starts up we make people smile and cool them down.'

Now you know how to get to your eternal home. Make people laugh! Build them up. Tell them they're clever, or good-looking, or kind. Buy a notebook to write down jokes!

But that remark about light entertainment still rankles. Some silly joke indeed! Well, here's one I heard in Berlin about pretentious holy people.

After the recent political changes, a holy man from the East made

'Before beginning my sermon I have something interesting to tell you.'

his first visit to the West. 'Have you any criticisms of the West?' the reporters asked deferentially. 'Yes,' he said. 'Two – I don't like know-alls!' They were intrigued. 'And the second criticism?' they enquired.

'I can't stand smarties,' he said. 'I never know how you peel them.'

My family thinks this is an awful joke, but I hope it makes you smile – because I want to go to heaven too, with you readers of course and those buskers.

To cure stress, anger, aggression, flus, fevers, rows and breakdowns, my grandmother prescribed 'Jewish Penicillin' – chicken soup. I do not have her recipe, but my friend Kim has given me his and it hits the right memories. Here it is. I call it Jewish-Gentile Penicillin.

Jewish-Gentile Penicillin –Kim's Chicken Soup

1 3lb (1.35kg) chicken with
  giblets
1 onion, finely chopped
2 pints (1.2 litres) water
1 large onion, finely chopped

1 tablespoon flour
¼ pint (150ml) single cream
  (or non-dairy substitute)
salt and pepper

● Season the chicken and roast it, stuffed with the onion, in a 'Rosta' bag if you have one. At the same time, simmer the giblets to make a stock.

● When the chicken is cooked, pour off all the juices (through the vent hole in the 'Rosta' bag). Place this with the giblet stock and giblets in the fridge.

● Eat and enjoy the chicken!

● Later, take off the scraps of meat from the carcass to add to the soup, put the carcass in a large saucepan with the water and boil for a good hour.

● De-fat the refrigerated stock and use this fat to soften the second large onion. Add the flour, mix and pour in all the stock, from the carcass and from the giblets. Stir well and simmer for 20 minutes.

● Add the chopped meat and giblets and the cream or substitute. Check for seasoning.

My Friend Who Fused the Lights

A lot of people are not religious but still read religious books or listen to religious talks on the radio. I don't think card-carrying members of religious organisations have any monopoly on goodness, and I do think that atheists or agnostics who don't believe in God can still accept a spiritual dimension to life.

My own spiritual life was very influenced by an agnostic. I still keep his book by my bed, and try to practise its precepts. He was an unlikely sort of chap to be a religious guide, for he wasn't keen on Christians – or Jews for that matter. He thought they were both stubborn and unreasonable, which is true of course. Also they gave him trouble, because he was a Roman emperor trying to keep the world together, and he thought they were rocking the boat. His name was Marcus Aurelius and he lived in the second century AD.

Now what do I learn from him? Well, he said, 'Tell yourself every morning "Today I'm going to meet a fool, someone I won't trust and a bully." But remember if you had their nature, you'd be the same.'

This is useful stuff, and I often sit back in bed before I get up and think of the people I'm going to meet during the day. There's a friend of mine who is coming to dinner, and whom I know from experience is a disaster area. Last time he came he stepped on my dog's tail, who barked and bounded backwards, hitting me just as I was holding a hot frying pan. In the confusion, the cooker came apart and the lights fused. My friend assured me he knew about fuses, stood on a chair, got a shock, and fell flat on my dining room table into the trifle I'd decorated so carefully. I sent the guests home, he went to the doctor, the dog went to the vet, and I retired to bed suffering from non-electric shock.

But after reading my Roman emperor I am now forewarned and forearmed, and I don't lose my cool, because I realise my friend can't do any different – for that's how he's made. So I make a picnic, instead of a dinner party, with finger food on paper plates and ban all beasts. I know his nature, you see, and accept it. It really helps if you rehearse difficult meetings in tranquillity, before they happen.

Another saying of Marcus Aurelius I like is 'Make for yourself a temple of quietness inside you.' Because of the insurance, lots of places of worship are now permanently locked, and much more difficult to get into than a bank. But if the church or synagogue or temple is in your mind, you can enter its peace, even while sitting on a bus, or even better on a park bench. 'Ah,' you say, 'what's all this about temples? I thought you said Marcus Aurelius wasn't a believer?' Well, he wasn't quite. He wrote, 'If there is a God, follow him, and if there isn't, be Godlike yourself.'

I used to know a rabbi who said there was a spiritual reason for the creation of everything. 'So why was the telephone created?' we asked him. 'To show you that what you say here is heard up there,' he replied.

And the railway?

'To teach you that delaying a minute can cost you everything.'

And why was atheism created? We thought we had him there.

'To teach you that if someone comes to you in need you shouldn't fob him off and say, "God will look after you." But you must act as if God didn't exist, and only you in the whole of creation could help him.'

Marcus Aurelius like all soldiers and generals had to eat on the trot since he must have spent most of his time on a horse. A bowl of soup is a most convenient stirrup cup, and this is what I would have eaten in his place.

Cullen Skink

12oz (350g) onion, roughly chopped
¾ pint (425ml) water
1lb (450g) haddock, smoked and undyed
1lb (450g) potatoes
¾ pint (425ml) skimmed milk
salt and freshly ground black pepper

• In a large saucepan, add the onions to the water and bring to a simmer. Lay the haddock on top of the onions and poach until cooked.

• Remove the fish and when cool flake the flesh; return the backbone to the onion if using fish on the bone. Continue simmering until the onion is just cooked; remove the backbone and return the flaked fish to the onions and water.

● Meanwhile, boil the potatoes in another saucepan. Mash roughly – it's nice to leave little lumps.

● Now carefully combine all the ingredients, add plenty of black pepper and a little salt, and pour in the skimmed milk.

● Leave until you are ready to eat and then heat very slowly until it begins to burp. Serve.

● Some people add cream, others crisply fried smoked meat, others croûtons. All of these detract from the excellence of this best of all chowders. The only thing I'd add if I had it, and the energy, would be a little chopped parsley at the last minute.

It freezes well for a short time.

If you cannot get undyed haddock do not attempt to make the Skink.

Patient Survival

When I was in hospital I was told I shouldn't work but take life easy.
Read light literature, they said, nothing that causes strain. Well, I tried
to read light literature, and found I couldn't cope with very much of it.
I enjoyed two love stories with happy endings but then I'd had
enough.

Cookery books rescued me. The recipes were just the right length,
and though I didn't want to *taste* the result, I made a meal of the idea of
it. Cookery was also a good subject of conversation with visitors. Now,
it's very nice having visitors, and reassuring; but you still have to
entertain them, even if you're cocooned in drips and drains and
festooned with wires and monitors.

The best way to keep them quiet is to get them to consume their
own presents. They will usually do this after a little urging – with a few
protests, such as: 'It doesn't seem right, does it, dear, eating the grapes
I got for you . . . well, I'll try one to please you . . . they really are
rather nice, aren't they?' And then they eat the lot! This makes me
happy! I like looking at people enjoying their food and while they are
munching I don't have to make conversation.

Just holding hands lightly is all a sick person wants. A simple action
like that reassures and comforts convincingly. But don't clutch or go
on too long. It's not so convincing if you overdo it.

Also, if you're a visitor, when do you leave? It's the same problem as
saying goodbye to someone on a railway platform. Do you just stand
there mouthing goodbyes through the glass like a goldfish? Do you
give up and go away? Well, I still can't solve the railway platform
dilemma but my tip to visitors is simple. When the patient yawns, say
goodbye nicely and go.

A friend of mine who is inspired by all the new Far Eastern cookery
gave me his own Anglo version of a Chinese soup when I was ill, and at
night I mulled it over in my mind.

Anglo-Chinese Soup

1½ pints (850 ml) good light
chicken stock
1 carrot, roughly chopped
1 onion, roughly chopped
1 stick of celery, roughly
chopped
1 teaspoon chilli sauce
2 dessertspoons anchovy
essence

12 peeled prawns *or* 4oz (110g)
white fish, flaked
1 tablespoon dry vermouth
finely sliced celery, red pepper
and leeks
salt and pepper

● Boil the carrot, onion and celery in the stock to add flavour. Strain, cool and de-fat.

● Add to the stock the rest of the ingredients, including a good handful of the vegetables. Adjust the seasoning according to your taste and serve at once so that the vegetables are still crisp.

Fish

In Jewish tradition, the righteous are destined to dine with God, wearing crowns of piety. Milk and honey will be provided, and there must be wine. The starters and puddings are not described, but the main dish, tradition asserts, will be leviathan, though how cooked it does not say. Leviathan is mentioned in the Bible and it is fishy. I imagine it as a giant conger eel, though conger eels are not kosher.

It is certainly true that Jewish cooking prefers fish. Perhaps because it is good for brains. And I prefer Jewish fish to all others. Cold fried fish is not a pleasant thought, but cooked à la juive, a tray of it is the tempting centrepiece of a Jewish Sabbath. And if you do not believe me, get yourself invited, and taste for yourself. It is eaten with grated beetroot and horseradish in white vinegar.

Non-Jewish stories are more descriptive of hell than heaven, and any food served (the fish of Hieronymous Bosch?) will cause problems of mastication and digestion. 'In that terrible day,' said the preacher solemnly, 'there will be groaning and gnashing of teeth!' 'But I haven't got any teeth,' exclaimed an old lady in the front pew. 'Teeth, madam,' replied the preacher firmly and politely, 'will be provided.'

Cheer Up and Bake a Pie

During certain periods of my life I am subject to panics which hit me most in the morning. I worry about a problem at the office, or a telephone call I have to make – small stuff, but not pleasant when you've lost your sense of proportion. I can get myself out of the house, but I still need cheering up. Now I prefer natural means to pills, and these are the ways I have found helpful. I'm setting them down because lots of other people have the same problem.

Start the day with a useful, undemanding task. I match single socks, and when I've made my first pair, I feel more optimistic about my prospects.

In my prayers I don't think about my faults and failures, which are only too evident, below as well as on high. I thank God for my successes and the fact that I'm here – I've survived! I also thank God for my first cup of tea. When I've managed to make that, I am over the worst.

I don't want to dive into my office and all its busy business straight away, so I give myself time to dawdle on my way there and this becomes the best time of the day.

There's always a warm welcome in charity shops. The ladies (and the occasional male) are friendly and have a good line in backchat. It's interesting, though a little sad, sorting through the debris of other people's lives, but it's fascinating. Also there's all the pleasure of the hunt, for surely there must be a bargain in that box of rubbish if only one could see it.

But alas, prices are going up in charity shops like everywhere else. I heard a man complaining about the price of a used Paris silk tie. He said he had always bought such ties for 15p and now they had gone up to 20p. What was the world coming to!

If even charity shops don't make you feel better, then why not have a second breakfast in a cheery transport café, eating all the things you don't admit to, liked baked beans with brown sauce, and strong stewed tea with three lumps of sugar.

A friend gave me this recipe for a comforting fish pie – which is an excellent dish to come home to. Even if you're nervy, it's problem-proof. I replace the prawns with the same quantity of tinned tuna.

Fish Pie

4 smoked haddock fillets –
   approximately ¾lb
   (350g)
1 pint (570ml) milk
2oz (50g) butter
1½oz (40g) flour
3 tablespoons anchovy essence

4oz (110g) peeled prawns (or
   tinned tuna)
4 eggs, hardboiled and coarsely
   chopped
1½lbs (675g) potatoes
salt and pepper

● Poach the haddock fillets in the milk. Skin and chop the fish –
don't lose the texture – and reserve the milk.

● Make a white sauce with the butter, flour and milk and season
with pepper and anchovy essence – the sauce will taste salty but this
should disappear so don't worry.

● Boil and mash the potatoes.

● Mix the fish and the sauce together with the prawns or tuna and
chopped eggs in a pie dish and top with mashed potato. Put in the oven
at Gas 3/325°F/160°C for 30 minutes, then cook for a further 10
minutes at Gas 6/400°F/200°C to brown the top.

● This recipe multiplies or divides well: 4 people, 4 fillets, 4 eggs, 4oz
(110g) prawns or tuna.

P . . . P . . . P . . .

When I came into the world cocooned in black hair, my mother exclaimed 'My God! He looks like the Devil!' At which her mother, whose only grandchild I was, had to be restrained from assaulting her. 'He's an angel!' she shouted. 'P . . . p . . . p . . . '. Not long after, my mother was rushed back to hospital with a rare blood illness, and I was brought up by granny. It was a love match and we educated each other.

While she pored over the pictures in my *Beano* and *Dandy*, I interpreted the balloons of text above Tiger Tim and Billy Bunter, over whose sad fate she wept, slow, Slav tears. In return, she fed me strudel and chicken giblets and instructed me in the ways of devils and demons, about which, coming from Eastern Europe, she knew a lot.

Demons lurked everywhere, in loos, behind doors and under beds. They were a spiteful lot, so if you said something nice about someone you spat three times – p . . . p . . . p . . . – to put them off. An amulet or a head of garlic also helped. To confuse them further you said the opposite of what you meant. 'E's a 'orrible kid,' said Granny gloating over me, eyes alight with love – 'P . . . p . . . p . . .' Oh, Granny, you confused me as well as the demons, and compliments are still a puzzle.

I thought of her last week when a friend returned from a visit to the shabby hamlet in Eastern Europe from which his family had fled. The old synagogue was now a store, for the Jews had gone long ago – the lucky ones to America, the unlucky ones to Auschwitz. An old crone, swathed in shawls, had followed him round the village, keeping a safe distance, peering at him round corners, and fluttering her hand at him. He imitated her, and I recognised the horns Granny made to protect me against the evil eye. The old woman thought the ghosts of the Jews were returning to reclaim their own, and she was frightened they'd reclaim her hovel. It had holes in the walls, and the wood was peeling away, but it was all she had.

Demons do exist, but they're inside us not outside. They're the ghosts of the wrongs we suffered, and the wrongs we inflicted. They're our bad memories, our guilt, and our fear of each other. They once took over whole countries in Europe, and still infest places like

Transylvania. They work openly in Northern Ireland, and the Middle East, and secretly in us.

Before religious festivals, people spring-clean the dirt from their houses. They should also wash the demons out of their minds, using courage and love in place of cleaning powder. Scriptures say 'God casts out demons'. Let him have a go at yours. 'P . . . p . . . p . . . '

My grandmother at first thought canned foods were the mark of the devil. But later on she succumbed, first to tinned salmon (to which she was partial) and then to tinned anchovies. A friend of mine helped me recreate her canned salmon cakes, as she never cooked by quantities and only scribbled notes in White Russian-Yiddish.

Granny's Salmon Fish Cakes

Makes 8

1lb (450g) tin of pink salmon (and its juice)

1 medium onion, finely chopped

2 eggs

4 heaped tablespoons medium Matzo meal

4 tablespoons chopped fresh parsley

salt and pepper

oil for frying

● Using a fork, mix together all the ingredients with four tablespoons of liquid from the tin of salmon (make up with milk if necessary). Keep some of the salmon texture.

● Wet your hands and shape into cakes. Coat with extra Matzo meal.

● Fry on both sides until brown.

Waiting

There are certain religious problems that once worried theologians and mystics, but that aren't much debated now. One of them concerned sexual thoughts in prayer. What do you do if you can't help thinking of a beautiful woman during a service? The traditionalists favoured a bucket. Fill it with ice water, keep it by your pew, and when you think of that beautiful woman pour it over your head. Two buckets should do the trick, three if you're young and impetuous!

The mystics were more subtle. 'Think of that beautiful woman even harder,' they said. 'Then think of all beautiful women. Then think of the beauty they have in common. Then add to it all the beauty in art, nature or goodness. Then think where beauty comes from, and so bring your thought back to God who'll purify it.' This way takes more time than the bucket, but you don't catch cold.

I used something similar when I waited for ten hours in an airport because of a strike. The departure lounge was blue with cigarette smoke, one traveller was drunk and some were sick. I didn't feel too well myself, consumed not by thoughts of sex, but of self-pity.

I wondered how they could do such things to me. Then I saw two old people sharing a single seat and a wave of real pity washed over me, which included me, them, a bawling baby and the defeated cleaners. Like a martyr, I queued for coffee, and returned queasy but content. By including others in my self-pity, God had got in, too, raising it like yeast and purifying it.

Now there may be a long hard summer ahead, with over-crowded airports and worry about strikes and travel companies collapsing. How are you going to purify your hurt feelings as you wait for a plane that may not come, or ask for a lift and get fobbed off? I recommend the following humbler ways from personal experience.

My mother turned hard times into a treat by making banana sandwiches and sharing them. Now Dame Julian the mystic wrote 'all will be well and all will be exceedingly well'. Well, my mother was no mystic – just a business woman who tried to make that happy ending come true. Julian would have liked her.

Some friends introduced me to Tai Chi exercises, which make me feel peaceful and amuse my fellow travellers.

And from my hitch-hiking days, *Pilgrim's Progress* taught me that my road led to heaven as well as to Calais, so I didn't hate the cars that didn't stop quite so much.

And in the old London smog, humour dissolved our irritation as we crashed into each other. And if you've got transport problems, here's a little tale to help you on.

As the cars are pouring into London, an old lady tries to cross the traffic at Marble Arch and is nearly knocked down by a car. 'Next time you jolly well look where you're going!' shouts the angry driver. The old lady trembles. 'Oh, sir, are you coming round again?' Well, God go with you. You need never wait alone.

My mother is a great secretary but has little time for cooking, though when she gives it her attention the result can be surprisingly good, even gastronomic. I have given her this recipe for Omelette Hilda Lessways. It's the perfect supper dish for a busy lady with little time.

Omelette Hilda Lessways

For each person

3 eggs
2 tablespoons cooked and flaked smoked haddock
salt and freshly ground black pepper

fresh chopped parsley
large knob of butter

● Whisk the eggs together with a little salt and plenty of black pepper.

● Melt a little of the butter in a saucepan and add the smoked haddock to warm it through.

● Melt the remaining butter in an omelette pan or a frying pan. Tip in the eggs and whilst the bottom of the omelette is warming up sprinkle the fish on to the still-wet centre. Cook until the middle is just moist but still juicy.

● Fold in half and serve, sprinkled with parsley, with plenty of good bread and a salad.

Waiter! Waiter!

After studying theology I knew a lot about God, not much about human beings and even less about myself. I considered myself a devout chap who wanted to devote his life to the service of his fellow human beings.

Well, I got my chance to serve them when I took a vacation job as a waiter. Ration books had just gone out and fancy restaurants were in, serving stewing steak and Cod Provençale with tinned toms and a packet of mixed herbs. After two days, I was dropping with exhaustion, my feet were sore, I had no high opinion of my customers either, who were as silly as hens and responsible for their own misery. They always wanted what wasn't on the menu.

'Waiter, I insist on fresh garden peas!' 'What could be fresher, moddom, than fresh, frozen, garden peas?' Then they always ordered the same thing at the same time, so there was never enough to go round. They wanted chicken breasts, but never legs or wings. Well, God doesn't grow birds that way, but would they believe it? Some customers slipped away without leaving a tip, some acted out their ego games, using me as their prop. I suffered in silence, trying to love them, but my soul became more sore than my feet. They made me so angry I couldn't sleep. A kind waitress took pity on me. 'Don't bottle it up, boy,' she said. 'It's better out than India,' which was wise advice.

So when a businessman used me as an Aunt Sally to amuse his guests, I retaliated with this story.

A businessman orders a fish in a restaurant, and is about to fillet it when the fish opens its glassy eye and sadly says, 'Don't eat me, mister!' The diner shudders, retches, and pushes his plate away. Next day he goes to a different restaurant and again orders fish. Just as he's about to dig in, the fish opens its eye, gazes at him wearily and says, 'Nice to see you again, mister. I didn't think the other restaurant was so hot either.'

The guests were amused, but it put my businessman off his Poisson Provençale. He ordered chopped liver instead. To my surprise he left me a large tip, and was the first customer I got to like. I got to like the others too, after I learnt three lessons very important for pious people, which you only learn from life.

'Which of you gentlemen ordered coffee in a clean cup?'

First – being a doormat is different from being devout. It doesn't help you, or the people you allow to tread on you.

Second – if you suppress your anger it will only boomerang back at you with migraines and depressions. The waiters taught me to express it, but not too heavily and with good humour.

Third – loving humanity is easy. But liking its individual specimens is jolly hard work. You learn a lot when you also serve and stand all day and wait.

The following fish supper is simple to prepare after you have been standing about all day – and that's the best ingredient of all.

Granny's Baked Fish

4 medium white fish fillets,
with skin
1 tin condensed cream of
smoked salmon soup

1 small tin peas (petit pois are
even better), drained
4oz (110g) mushrooms, sliced
1 teaspoon sherry

- Place the fish fillets skin side down in a greased baking dish.

- Mix together the cream of smoked salmon soup (don't add any liquid), the peas, the mushrooms and the teaspoon of sherry (no more). Pour over the fish and bake for 25 minutes at Gas 3/325°F/160°C.

- If you can't find cream of smoked salmon soup, cream of celery would do well.

England, Oh, My England

'My dear,' I heard one elderly lady say to my mother, 'they're simply ruining the place.'

'Nonsense!' said my mother cheerfully. 'They're putting up new blocks of flats everywhere!'

Well, that's the difference! You can either sigh for an old England or you make your peace with the new one we've got and find out how to enjoy it.

As a youngster I was sure that bliss could only be obtained by the side of the Mediterranean, and I hopefully decorated my kitchen with empty Chianti bottles and strings of expensive onions I had bought from Bretons on bicycles.

After a while the bottles and onions, of course, looked a little tired and dusty. The general effect, with a bit of imagination, was supposed to provoke thoughts of St Rafael or Rimini. But now my taste has changed. I want to discover my own country instead – take a canal boat through the strange and sumptuous industrial scenery of the Midlands, wander down a Yorkshire dale, or stumble upon a hidden village with its church, chapel, and rose garden. I also want to come to terms with the other Englands, the ones the tourist brochures don't bother about.

There is a strange new gastronomic England that has begun to take shape – sometimes gorgeous and exotic, occasionally gruesome. It's the exotic world of take-aways! You can get chop suey and chips from a Chinese kitchen situated conveniently by the parish church.

Curry on toast is also common and convenient, and be a hamlet ne'er so humble, it can usually provide a pizza, a taco, or some other finger-lickin' far-flung product.

The mixture is mind-blowing but one day the stew out of which this country is composed – Saxons, Normans, Celts and Norsemen, all simmering nicely together, with a few Romans and Hebrews thrown in for flavour – will absorb the new exotics. I lick my lips as I think of the menus that will emerge from that mixture.

There's also an England of good deeds, which doesn't get the limelight it deserves. I'm thinking of the nice nuns who run coffee stalls for the down-and-outs near the docks, of the church crypts which shelter the forlorn with hospitality and humour, and the people in voluntary organisations who give their time to those with problems without counting the minutes or the money.

There is an army of God's workers helping alcoholics, AIDS victims, and drug sufferers. You won't find their names or the place where they work in any brochure, but in God's eyes they are the glory of this country. In fact, I don't think I've ever been in a country where so much voluntary work is done, and there are so many things going wrong that it's nice to hand out well-deserved bouquets!

Now here's an exotic way of cooking the staple fare of the English family — fish fingers!

Exotic Fish Fingers

1lb (450g) fish fingers
2oz (50g) butter or margarine
2 tablespoons anchovy essence
½ hot green chilli pepper,
    deseeded and chopped
2 cloves of garlic, crushed
4 tablespoons oil, preferably
    olive

● In a frying pan, melt the butter with all the other ingredients except for the fish fingers. Sizzle gently for a few minutes.

● Now add the fish fingers to the mixture — it will certainly wake them up! Fry until cooked through and brown, and serve with the cooking sauce poured over, chilli and all.

The Elegant Woman

At school I learned to read books, but my mother taught me to read people. So like her I sit in cafés, and on concourses, considering them and the human condition.

Which is why, when taken to lunch in Central Europe, to a restaurant quite out of my class, I couldn't concentrate on my artichoke stuffed with mousse but fed my eyes on the two people at the next table instead.

The man, commented my French host, was a *vieux beau*, an old *roué* – though of the respectable sort, a common type in his own country. He wore designer clothes, and gold winked discreetly from his hands and wrists and the silver hairs, carefully but casually arranged around his throat. He talked non-stop, totally absorbed in himself and his gestures, only distracted by a particularly fat oyster, or a fine fig bursting with juice.

I decided he was a bore, and concentrated on his companion instead. I couldn't calculate her age. Her flawless enamelled look defeated me, only betrayed by one faintly greasy patch, where she had over-applied her foundation cream. As in a mosaic, her outlined eyes under thin arched lines looked into some remote distance. She nodded briefly two or three times and once signed to the waiter for more wine and oysters. She too gleamed with gold, and winked with diamonds.

Our tables were decently spaced, so my companions and I could discreetly discuss the pair. Surely, they said, there was a sermon in them? Were they married, for example? And did it matter? With clerical consent or without it, the terms of their relationship were quite clear. He provided her with diamonds and oysters, and she provided him with sex, status, and something elegant to look at, whenever he paused for breath, which was admittedly not often. It was an arrangement not uncommon in Continental countries where a mistress could be wined and dined in public without comment.

We watched as the head waiter showed the couple to their car. And then my *vieux beau* stumbled, and for a second a look of mingled passion and pity tore apart the wrinkle-free face of his companion. It passed in a flash, lest it leave tell-tale lines. She glanced our way for a moment and I cringed.

Suddenly I knew my sermon and its message. Look at people if you like, but never judge them! You're not God. You can't see into their hearts, and you'll get them wrong. Judging others is a sin religious people are particularly prone to, and my first major one since my last great repentance. I am really rather ashamed.

Now, I am not into oysters, and the homely cooking of this book is not in the elegant lady's class. If she ever employed me, which I doubt, I would prepare trout very simply for her and her companion. Roger Royle told me how, and in his honour I call the result . . .

Trout Royale

Serves 2

2 fresh rainbow trout, washed   herbs of your choice
   and cleaned   1 lemon
1oz (25g) butter

● Place the fish side by side in a buttered ovenproof dish; dot with some small pieces of butter and sprinkle with herbs. (I have a bag of herbs from Provence that I find very useful.) Top each fish with a generous slice of lemon and cover.

● Bake in the oven at Gas 4/350°F/180°C for about 30 minutes. Roger cooks them in the microwave for 5–6 minutes at high power.

● Discard the lemon cooked with the fish and serve with fresh lemon slices.

Practise As You Preach

If you drop in on another religion you always feel a bit uneasy. There are so many hidden traps. When do you sit down or stand up? When people go to the altar or ark, do you join in companionably or sit glued to your seat in the back row, looking standoffish? Whatever you do seems wrong or rude. It's a problem, and I've seen lots of people wondering whether they've got the courage to go in.

Of course, the texts outside tell you about loving each other and all of you being sisters and brothers together, but we've learned to take official words with a pinch of salt. It's easy to talk about loving mankind, but difficult to welcome one stranger.

I wandered into a strange church a few weeks ago because I wanted to say a prayer for a friend of mine who had died. It seemed her sort of place. I said a prayer for her, but I felt an outsider as everyone lined up for Communion and I sat on, a stranger in a strange place. I tried to hurry away but I was waylaid by a woman who ushered me into the church hall and put a cup of tea in one of my hands, and a big slice of cake in the other. 'Come on, lovey,' she said, 'eat it up, we're not as bad as all that. I made the cake myself, and I'm not one to count the currants.'

Another sort of service took place in the church hall, not as formal as the first, but with the same features if you could spot them. This time, ladies ministered to me, not handing out hymnals, but buns and biscuits. And because they gave them with a good heart it was a kind of cosy kitchen communion with lots of calories. The old minister from the church came up to me, too, and refreshed my cup.

He didn't preach about kindness, he just did me a kindness. It was the best sermon of all.

I couldn't participate in everything of course, even there. The lady said: 'Have a slice of meat pie. I made it myself.' 'I can't,' I said, 'because I'm Jewish.'

'Well, that's a real shame,' she said. 'It's one of my best.' 'Never mind,' I said, and I confided in her what my old grandpa used to say: 'Lionel, if you're a pious Jew in this world, God might let you live like a gentile in the next.'

I have always found this fish recipe easy and appropriate for strangers who suddenly appear for dinner in my home (not in a place of worship).

Sister Lucy's Haddock au Gratin

4 haddock fillets	*Topping*
1 onion, chopped	**3 or 4 Weetabix biscuits,**
1 green pepper, deseeded and sliced	**crushed, or cornflakes or crisps**
1 tomato, chopped	**2oz (50g) peanuts or other nuts,**
2oz (50g) mushrooms	**roughly crushed**
	2oz (50g) grated cheese

1½oz (40g) butter
1oz (25g) flour } *or* 1 can condensed cream of mushroom soup
¾ pint (425ml) milk
salt and pepper

● Fry together the onion and green pepper, tomato and mushrooms for 2–3 minutes.

● Make a white sauce with the butter, flour and milk (or open and heat the can of mushroom soup), and add a little of the cheese. Stir into this the onion, pepper, tomato and mushroom mixture.

● Place the fish fillets in a casserole dish and pour the sauce over them. It should just cover the fish (too much and the topping will sink into it).

● Mix together the topping ingredients and spread over the fish and the sauce.

● Bake in a moderate oven, Gas 4/350°F/180°C, for about 20 minutes.

Fashion and Fun

I've been thinking about holidays again. Before the war, holidays meant Margate – the only place outside London I visited until the Blitz blew all our lives into unfamiliar trajectories.

I don't actually mean Margate of course, which was not gentle or genteel enough for us, but Cliftonville, its quieter suburb. Gentility is not high on the list of priorities in upper middle-class Hampstead or Highgate. And in really upper-class districts it is consciously avoided, for modish and modified punk is the regulation uniform and style in the stylish streets around London's central parks.

But for lower middle-class East Enders, who were hanging by a thread over the abyss of unemployment and bailiffs, gentility was all. No let-up was allowed. Manners maketh man, and they helped us to cling to our clawhold on the social ladder.

So we visited Margate, Southend and Brighton. But for gentility we lodged in Cliftonville, Westcliff, and Hove, their dull but demure attendant suburbs.

Hotels were, of course, beyond our reach, though very distant cousins who had 'made it' stayed in them (or so I was told). We stayed, instead, in the little boarding-houses. There were whole streets of these, sloping away from the beach to the outskirts. They had only tiny front gardens for prestige, so you could see straight through the bow windows into the dining-rooms, where tables crowded against each other, and there were bottles of brown sauce, red sauce, and pickles.

For my mother and her sisters the big event was their début on the promenade. For a whole year they had debated the pros and cons of beach pyjamas. Did one dare risk it? (Once again, the social pit below opened up, disclosing its dreadful jaws.)

Each year had its own fashion. One year it was cellophane necklaces, and another it was Donald Duck jewellery and pendants. In 1937 people asked each other: 'Why did the chicken cross the road?' (Answer below.) And in 1938 they 'Lambeth walked' and shouted, 'Oy!'

Some years the ladies looked like *femmes fatales* and slunk along the beach, and some years they all looked like extras from the *White Horse Inn* and wore dirndls.

On those holidays, I became a 'man of the world' – pint sized. It was the first time I tasted spaghetti not out of a tin, and I was very proud. Here it is with an uncommon sauce.

Pasta with Cauliflower Sauce

1lb (450g) macaroni or other pasta

Sauce
1 large cauliflower
3 tablespoons olive oil
1 large onion, chopped
2 cloves of garlic, crushed
1 dessertspoon anchovy essence
salt and freshly ground black pepper
red cheese, grated

● Separate the cauliflower into florets; keep some chopped stalk but throw away the leaves. Boil until just tender, drain thoroughly and mash, saving some small whole florets.

● Boil the pasta for about 12 minutes, rinse and drain.

● Meanwhile, heat the oil in a pan and sauté the onion and garlic until soft. Add the mashed cauliflower and anchovy essence and fry gently for a few minutes, adding pepper and salt (remembering that the anchovy is already quite salty).

● Pour over the pasta and sprinkle with red cheese and the whole cauliflower florets.

(Answer: To get to the other side, of course. In 1937, people suspected a war was coming and needed any laugh.)

Templing and Tombing

With an innocent air, I urge my friend Fred to drive faster – which he does and so shoots past the Dog and Duck and misses his lunch. It's a dirty trick and exactly what I intended.

Fred is furious. 'I'll never go on holiday with you again, Lionel! I can't abide your "templing and tombing". It isn't natural busting into shrines on holiday. You ought to be oiling yourself on a beach. In any case, what's a Yiddisher boy like you messing around with monks for? You're not C of E like me. You ought to be thinking about kosher fish cakes not Saxon saints on short rations. Anyway, you've already done this St Wulfstan before – in Worcester – I never thought you'd sink, Lionel, to recycling saints.'

My professional pride is hurt. 'I'm not!' I burst out indignantly. 'I'm not recycling St Wulfstan of Worcester, you clot, but St Walston on the way to the Wash.'

Fred sees red, and I persuade him to pull up by a supermarket in case we crash. While he contemplates brands of cooling beer, I go 'templing and tombing', and locate my shrine in a sort of potting shed, hidden away behind a housing estate.

In it there's room for me, some candles and the usual pious knick-knacks. I relax into its peace and hope eternity will touch me. Because unless it does, our holiday just won't work. Fred can't understand it, but I can only cope with this world if I keep my grip on the next. If I know my eternal home isn't here I get less grumpy about hotels. Even if the bathwater does overflow into the bidet – that's better than the other way round. Perfection is in another place.

And in this shrine I know this world alone can't provide the happiness I want. Breasts, bulges and bottoms on a beach are a turn-on, it's true, and if you pretend not to notice you look furtive not pious. But for love, a shrine is better than a beach.

And it's the same with comfort. On its own it isn't enough. I need contentment, too. But no package holiday can provide that, only prayer.

I look around the shrine and its exotic icons. Fred's right – religious dogmas don't cross religious frontiers, but he's wrong too, because religious experience does. After all, you don't have to be Jewish to enjoy kosher fish cakes.

Fish cakes! The holiness which inhabits the shrine reminds me Fred's been waiting an awful long time for lunch. I stand him a salmon sandwich at the next pub to say sorry. 'You're your nice natural self once more, Lionel,' he says, which makes me mad all over again, because I'm not nice naturally, only supernaturally. But this, Fred, who is *naturally* nice, will never understand. Perhaps he doesn't have to.

When we got home, I made him these kosher fish cakes. They're too good for tomato sauce and convenience chips. They deserve new potatoes and petit pois and so of course do you.

Kim Holman's Fish Cakes

Makes 10

1½lbs (675g) haddock fillets, skinned and boned
1 medium onion, peeled
1 medium potato, peeled
1 tablespoon caster sugar
1½ tablespoons salt
¼ teaspoon white pepper
9 heaped tablespoons fine Matzo meal
2 tablespoons vegetable oil
2 eggs, beaten
oil for deep-frying

● Chop the haddock finely in a food processor. Transfer to a bowl and then put the onion and potatoes through the processor.

● Strain the chopped onion and potato and add to the fish, reserving the juice. Now add to this mixture the sugar, salt, pepper, 4 tablespoons of the Matzo meal and oil. Gently mix everything together with the eggs, adding the onion juice if the mixture seems a bit dry. Leave to rest for an hour or so in the fridge.

● Wet your hands and form the mixture into fish cakes. Dredge in the rest of the Matzo meal.

● Deep-fry in oil for about 7 minutes, turning gently. Drain.

Meat

Meat, I confess, is a problem, especially for a cook who wishes to combine it with spirituality. Once it was a ritual problem, now it is a moral, and, alas, for me a medical problem.

Rationally, my moral problem is concerned with killing and even more with battery-living. Not so rationally, it came to a head in a hotel with a New Year's buffet. The centrepiece was a whole lamb, roasted, with one red eye and one green, which winked electrically at the diners. I have remained an on—off, half-vegetarian ever since.

Vegetarianism, like all worthy things, can be used for base and unworthy purposes, such as righteous indignation and one-upmanship, spiritual pride, and disguised aggression. Hitler was a vegetarian, too. I rarely cook meat now, but I eat it when I am served it at restaurants, banquets, and in other people's homes. Apart from battery veal, I enjoy it. If I should ever encounter an ox, that had lived a long, rich life and died with a smile on its lips, I would be tempted to stew its tail — with wine, or beer and butter beans.

Occasionally I cook meat for friends and family, and, though I cannot enjoy much myself (cholesterol), I enjoy their enjoyment.

If you can, get your meat and poultry free-range.

With woven vegi-chicken now, you sometimes get a plastic wishbone. It does not add to the taste, which is satisfactory, but it does add humour to a heavy subject.

Enjoy, enjoy!

How Does a Cow Emulate a Hare
or Going Dutch

There are two English meals worth showing off – breakfast and high tea. Dutch breakfasts also are memorable, though strange. I now enjoy aniseed balls on bread, and grated chocolate on bread, and even gingerbread on bread. They are substantial, and, in the last resort, I'm more of a peasant than a gourmet, and I prefer quantity to quality.

So I decided to give an old-fashioned English breakfast in Holland and invite my Dutch friends. There was cereal and milk and eggs and baked beans and what have you, and lots of time, which is the most delicious ingredient of all. So we sat round the table with the newspapers, and I tried to think Dutch.

Though Holland is our nearest and pleasantest neighbour, we don't think much about it. It isn't just tulips, dairy produce, and the Nightwatch in the flesh in central Amsterdam or in the Rijksmuseum on canvas. But I think the greatest achievement of the Dutch is friendship. Every country has its own form. In England there are infinite gradations of love to loathing, most of them hard to distinguish, because a gooey layer of politeness covers the lot. In Holland politeness is replaced by directness, which is unnerving but reassuring.

My Dutch friends are constant and caring. They meet me at the station when I arrive. Though I haven't seen them for years they remember my favourite foods, and provide me with small bottles of hot 'sambal', or a creamy 'green herring' on a soft roll. They never desert me when I need them, and they give me the advice I need to hear, which is not what I like to hear. And this last is the greatest friendship of all. My Dutch friends know what I am, and they accepted the package philosophically long ago.

But Dutch humour is a different story. At my breakfast party I said, 'Tell me a really Dutch joke.' After a long pause, someone volunteered.

'How does a cow emulate a hare?'

'Well, how does it?' I said helpfully.

'It stands under a tree,' my friend answered unhappily, 'and thinks about a cauliflower.'

I smiled politely and wondered if she was having me on. But it is an old Dutch joke, connected with an old Dutch proverb about hares and cows and cauliflower. I suddenly remembered the time I had tried to explain the Cockney alphabet in German. And I am always surprised when Jewish jokes go down well with gentiles.

Dutch recipes, now, are a different matter. There is a lot of pork in them, so I have to adapt them, because of my religious food regulations. Anyway, here is one given me by my Dutch friend Theo, with some Yiddish amendment.

Theo's Casserole

1lb (450g) cured meat, smoked, dried or salted
1lb (450g) smoked sausage
2oz (50g) butter or margarine
1lb (450g) onions, chopped
2 cloves of garlic, chopped
1 dessertspoon mild paprika
¼ pint (150ml) stock
2lb (900g) tinned sauerkraut
2 tablespoons tomato purée
½ teaspoon sugar
1 pint (570ml) cream or non-dairy cream substitute
salt and freshly ground pepper

● Melt the butter or margarine in a casserole and brown the meat and sausage. Add the onions and garlic and brown them too. Then add the paprika and stock and simmer very gently for about 1½ hours.

● Meanwhile, empty the sauerkraut into a saucepan and let it simmer for about 1 hour.

● Add the sauerkraut to the meat, along with the tomato purée and sugar, and let it all cook for another 30 minutes.

● Just before serving, stir in the cream or cream substitute, and season to taste. Heat through and serve with boiled potatoes, pasta or rice.

Minding Your Own Business

A businessman in my congregation used to come up to me and say, 'Rabbi Blue, I wouldn't have your job for the world.' I wanted to tell him, 'I wouldn't have yours, either,' but I never said it, because it sounded rude, and though I didn't mean it that way, it was true.

I never knew how they slept, the small-businessmen in my congregation. They had mortgaged homes, one and a half cars to keep up, and the same number of executive children to educate. It petrified me to see how their blossoming businesses were at the mercy of economic waves, which I never understood; and I don't think they did either, though they tried to explain them to me as well as to each other.

Businessmen (especially traders and credit operators) don't get a good press in the Bible, and, if you go into any place of worship, the places of honour are occupied by soldiers, sailors, saints, sinners (of the superior and repentant sort), mystics and crusaders. You don't often find their counterpart, the righteous businessman. Yet a lot of businessmen are very righteous and very generous.

As a minister you are often stuck for money. Whether a massive mortgage is collapsing or you need a voucher for a night at the Sally

'This illustrates what I've said time and time again. If you haven't got sufficient capital you don't start to build.'

Army for someone who is homeless and hopeless, a bit of money helps. I don't think the small traders in my congregations ever gave me a 'no' when I asked them in an emergency. After a hard week's work they went to Rotary, or Round Table, or Ladies' Circles to raise ever more money for charities.

I had my disagreements with them of course. They tended to think what was good for commerce was good for the cosmos too, and when they tried to fund my deficit with a Monte Carlo night some harsh words were said. (In any case, they got the odds for roulette wrong.)

The difficulty was explaining to them that the 'God business' is like no other, and its 'end product' is unquantifiable, and perhaps unmarketable by normal means. Like most of my congregation, they wanted to see results, and what are religious 'results' if you are not interested in real estate or throwing up a lot of buildings? Nearing OAP status, I am still trying to work that one out.

Businessmen, to my bewilderment, liked baby food or nursery nosh. They liked rice puddings (even tapioca), toad-in-the-hole, angels on horseback, bread and butter pudding and roly-poly. Whatever it was, they also liked a lot of it.

This recipe would suit them well. It's simple to prepare and has the touch of sweetness businesspeople crave. It can also be fingerfood, though it's messy. When I ran out of wine, I used a slurp of Coca-Cola, which worked fine.

Businesspeople's Chicken

2–3lb (900g–1.35kg) chicken	1 packet of French onion soup
1 large bottle of whole cranberry sauce	1 glass wine (any colour!)

- Joint the chicken and put the pieces in a baking dish.

- In a saucepan heat the cranberry sauce, packet of onion soup and the wine. When it's all melted together, pour the sauce over the chicken pieces, turning them about in it.

- Put the dish in the oven preheated to Gas 4/350°F/180°C and bake for 1 hour or until the chicken pieces are done.

- It's good with easy-cook rice.

Send an Old Friend a
Parcel of Memories

A friend of mine rang me from America and I asked her what she would like for Christmas. 'Well,' she said, 'we've got even more this side of the Atlantic than you.'

'Is there anything you've got less of?' I asked. 'Yes,' she replied. 'We haven't got as many memories.'

But how do you make a parcel of memories? I wondered.

Then I thought of a present I had been given a few years ago, and hardly ever used. It was a little portable tape-recorder. Why not make a cassette of memories, I thought, and send it to her. Well, I've done it and I think it's the best present I've ever given.

We used to know each other in childhood, so I've recalled streets that have disappeared, and school chums with whom we've lost touch. I remembered games we used to play, and skipping songs we used to jump to in the street. I found that I still remembered gas-lighters who came around with long poles, and the glow of their mantles – much more delicate than the harsh electric light that replaced them.

I suddenly thought how wonderful it would be if I had a cassette from my grandparents. They came from Russia at the turn of the century, and there can't be anything left of the little communities they left – the Nazis and their wars saw to that. How I would love to have memories of their world! I remember my grandmother saying how awesome electricity seemed – more impressive than any sermon she had heard. It was miraculous – you turned a little stick in the wall, and then there was light. Like Genesis, Chapter 1!

How I would love to have memories of relatives and friends – especially the former. There must be so many distant cousins who were lost to me. I know I've got some in America and Africa, but are there any left in Europe? God knows!

So my suggestion for a Christmas present that you can pass like an heirloom from generation to generation is a tape of your memories. It's beyond price.

A Christmas present that is priceless, but costs nothing except the paper it is written on, is a recipe. This one was given to me by my friend Kim, who comes from Cornwall. These pasties were our treats and comforters as we crossed the North Sea in a small boat.

Cornish Pasties

For 8 pasties

Pastry	Filling
1lb 6oz (625g) plain flour	14oz (400g) chuck steak, chopped small
8oz (225g) Cookeen	7oz (200g) ox kidney
4oz (110g) suet	1 medium onion, chopped
2 medium eggs, beaten	1 large potato, diced
6fl oz (200ml) water	¼ swede, diced
salt and pepper	8 tablespoons suet
1 beaten egg to glaze	salt and pepper

● First make the pastry: rub the cut-up fat into the flour and add the other ingredients, using as much of the water as you need to make a not-too-sticky dough.

● Divide the pastry into eight pieces and roll out each one into a round, using a plate to 'draw' round for an even shape.

● In the middle of each circle place in layers a portion of each item of filling, with the meat at the top. Don't overfill.

● Wet the circumference of the pastry with a pastry brush, bring the edges together over the centre of the filling and pinch to seal. Make two steam holes in the centre.

● Place on a greased baking tray and paint each pasty with beaten egg. Bake at Gas 6/400°F/200°C for 25 minutes and a further 25 minutes at Gas 3/325°F/160°C, until golden and cooked.

Religion and the Retail Trade

The lover in the Song of Songs likes to browse among the lilies at the bottom of his garden. I prefer the tinned tomatoes and baked beans in my local supermarket, for mild consumerism is as soothing as meditation.

I always assumed that baked beans just appeared, like crocuses in spring. But then I met the backroom boys who put them there and they proudly showed me their technology, computers and distribution systems. 'Our business isn't glamorous, Rabbi,' they said wistfully. 'It hasn't got any connection with yours.' But they did themselves an injustice, because God created us with souls and bodies, so we need both blessings and baked beans, religion and the retail trade to survive.

I remember the post-war years when baked beans were in short supply and Britishers then lived like East Europeans now. People said that well-stocked shelves in the shops would automatically make everybody kind and content, so spirituality and all that see-through stuff was redundant. And they were right – for a while! People were good, when they had never had it so good.

But in 1968 the big boom turned into a little bust, people changed from nice to nasty overnight, and racialism was revived. Good-time goodness without God just didn't have enough stamina. The hippies of course made the opposite mistake. They were for the spirit, and against business. Well, business just took them over and absorbed them into the pop and fashion industry.

Perhaps there will be another tight year ahead. High mortgage interest repayments may knock out that family holiday or new car. But just because business doesn't boom there's no need to turn nasty and make everybody else's life a misery. Let your body and soul help each other. Bring them together! If you remember your religion in the supermarket, and that 'man doesn't live by bread alone', you'll save yourself a lot of silly spending.

And when you're in church or synagogue, remember your material needs, and then you won't misuse religion for escapism, for you can't live on blessing alone either, and nor can others. Your body and soul can purify each other if you let them. And I suspect God made us a mixture of spirit and flesh for just that purpose. Not everything can be transferred, of course. One backroom boy asked me if the technology that made the distribution trade efficient would work for religion too.

Regretfully, no. Take that computer, for example, which could translate the scriptures into any modern language. Well, they fed in 'the spirit is willing but the flesh is weak'. And what did they get out – 'the gin is full strength but the beef is flabby'.

Well, if the beef isn't that good, mince and recreate it (nice word!) as a meat loaf. Meat loaf goes with baked beans. It is not always gastronomic but everyone has two helpings. This loaf is more gastronomic than most, using brandy, honey and herbs. I first had it at a dinner party given by the artist André Vogt.

Honey Meat Loaf

1lb (450g) lean minced beef	1 tablespoon brandy or sherry
1 egg	1 teaspoon salt
2 slices of white bread, soaked	¼ teaspoon pepper
in water, squeezed dry, and	1 dessertspoon clear honey
fluffed up with a fork	1 teaspoon mixed herbs

● Mix together all the ingredients except the honey and herbs and shape into a flattened ball. Place on a greased baking tray.

● Heat the honey with the herbs and spoon over the loaf. Bake for about an hour at Gas 3/325°F/160°C, basting occasionally.

A Stew is a Stew is a Stew . . .

Others commit sins. I shall commit a cookbook. 'But, Rabbi Blue, is a cookbook really necessary?' 'Of course not, silly! A stew is a stew is a stew, whether it's rump boiled in old Burgundy or an old boot in a beef cube. You put one herb in, you take another out, you crush a clove of garlic and you shake it all about.' As my colleague Rabbi Gryn says, 'No matter how you slice the salami, Lionel, it's still the same salami.'

But never in the field of human history have so many been so full and fixated on food. They don't just want to eat the stuff, they must read about it too.

I puzzled over the problem at the funeral of a nice old gent who met me each year to sort out some affairs. Instead of a cup of coffee, he insisted on dining me at an expensive eaterie quite out of my class. I couldn't choose the cheapest dish because it seemed insulting. The second ditto, and the third I could cook myself. The other prices soared into the stratosphere and made me much too edgy to enjoy anything. We both gave a sigh of relief as we left the restaurant and each other.

I brooded over the problem in the funeral chapel and the penny dropped. I knew why he invited me out. He couldn't stand me, but felt guilty about it, so he stuffed me instead. The meal was marvellous but tasteless, because it covered his lack of love.

It must be the same at those banquets when world leaders threaten each other politely with atom bombs over the petits fours. All that smoked salmon is a smoke screen which hides the horror and their lack of trust.

It's the same with me when I gorge from the fridge at night and never feel full. My belly feels hungry but it's my soul that's starved. The missing ingredient which makes any meal special isn't material, so you can't buy it in supermarkets. It's spiritual – and so you may have more luck in a church or a temple.

I have friends in Eastern Europe, who may be narked by all this dismissive talk about luxuries they've been denied so long. But I hope they don't change one crude materialism for another, because they can do without our drug culture and self-destructive greed. Western bananas, popcorn, and fizzy drinks are fine but not enough. They, too, lose their taste unless they're cooked with the milk of human kindness and served with a slice of the bread of heaven.

Now the following stew really is different because it uses no water or wine, only brown ale. It comes from Belgium, where the beer is brewed by monks and contemplatives and one pint of which would knock an ordinary British boozer flat. Good brown ale does nicely. This recipe also works, though not so well, with ordinary lager. Shin is fine as the alcohol and slow cooking tenderise it. It is a versatile dish and I have sometimes experimented by adding beans, Worcestershire sauce, anchovy essence, and dumplings. They all worked.

Carbonade

2lb (900g) shin, cut into chunks
3 tablespoons seasoned flour
2 tablespoons oil
1lb (450g) onions, chopped
3 cloves of garlic, crushed
  (optional)
1 dessertspoon tomato purée
1 pint (570ml) brown ale
1 dessertspoon French or
  German mustard

1 teaspoon brown sugar
5 fresh sage leaves *or* ½
  teaspoon dried sage
7 or 8 peppercorns
1lb (450g) carrots, cut into
  rounds
salt and freshly ground black
  pepper

● Roll the meat in the seasoned flour and brown quickly in hot oil in a casserole; remove with a slotted spoon.

● Soften the onions and the garlic in the oil and add the rest of the seasoned flour and the tomato purée. Cook gently, stirring to make sure it doesn't stick, then gradually pour in the ale to make a smooth sauce.

● Bring to a simmer and return the meat to the casserole, along with the mustard, sugar, sage, peppercorns, carrots and seasoning. Stir well.

● Cover the casserole and put into a preheated oven Gas 3/ 325°F/160°C for 3–4 hours. If after an hour it's simmering too fast, turn down to Gas 2/300°F/150°C. It should simmer gently.

● Accompany with jacket potatoes, which can be cooked on another shelf in the oven.

A Suitcase of Memories in Berlin

I never learnt the important things on formal college courses. A London backstreet before the war taught me the truths about my own nature – that I could be a bully and a delinquent – and a post-war London café the hard truths about religion. There I encountered refugees from the Weimar Republic who had once addressed great academies in Berlin and were now reduced to chatting to a teenage ignoramus like me. They were the first intellectuals I'd met, and their dedication to truth awed me.

One had just finished a weighty novel when he became convinced that its proper expression was a short story. Three hundred hand-written pages disappeared into the dustbin.

A musicologist of genius who had discovered that the human voice could encompass ten octaves and proved it, took me on as a pupil. (I thought it would make me more interesting at parties.) 'Make this note,' he said, sounding the top key on the piano. 'I can't,' I smirked. He picked me up, and hurled me at the wall. 'Make it,' he said and I did.

They made no objection when I took to religion – just warning me that tradition too is subject to truth, and doubt was divine – without it you can't tell the difference between faith and wish-fulfilment. In Hitler's Germany they had witnessed both. On the one hand Bonhoeffer and his confessing church. On the other, carols sung beside concentration camps.

In a shabby café in East Berlin I'll drink to their shades, though they left me a legacy of awkward questions I cannot wish away, though I've tried. If the Nazis had shot only gypsies and beheaded homosexuals, would rabbis too have stood aside? If Hitler, or Stalin, had conquered this country, how many Christian leaders would have compromised here? How can we know till we are tested if our religion is real?

The answer to the first two questions is speculation, but the third concerns us now, and in Berlin we know our answer can't be words, for there words were prostituted too many times to be trusted. 'In the West, man exploits his fellow man,' said an East German intellectual. 'And in the East?' 'Oh, here it's the other way around!' You can point this crack any way you like.

But if the question disturbs you enough, as it should, you can prove your religion real with your life. Just use your faith to increase your courage, kindness and passion for truth. For though truth is tough it makes you free, say the gospels – and according to the rabbis God said, 'If only people would forsake Me but keep My commandments.'

My intellectuals would have said, 'Ja, ja,' to both statements.

In Berlin I am always conscious of how close the Slav part of Europe is. It is reflected in the food, the fashions, the culture and the names. I always felt drawn eastwards to the Polish frontier, beyond which lay the home of my ancestors.

This recipe is Polish, which would be equally popular in Berlin – there is the same liking for gherkins, savouries, and smoked meat. Obviously you can add your own examples of the last – that's your affair! It was given to me by Krystyna Kaplan, who with her husband Jan directed me in the television series 'In Search of Holy England'. She is a beautiful, willowy blonde, who has made films on fashion, and once drove a truck. Her tiny kitchen is a generous Slavonic cornucopia.

Polish Beef Olives

Serves 4

4 thinly sliced beef pieces
  (large enough for stuffing
  with vegetables and
  frankfurters)
mustard
4 frankfurters, cut into strips
4 slices of smoked sausage
2 carrots, diced

4 gherkins, chopped
4 hardboiled eggs, sliced
2 tablespoons oil
1 onion, sliced
beef stock cube dissolved in a
  cup of hot water
1 tablespoon flour
salt and pepper

●   Beat each slice of meat lightly. Spread thinly with mustard, sprinkle with salt and pepper and arrange on top the frankfurters, smoked sausage, carrots, gherkins, and sliced egg. Roll each up and tie securely with thread.

●   Coat each beef olive with flour and fry in oil until golden. Place in a casserole.

●   Fry the sliced onion separately, and add to the casserole, with the beef stock. Simmer gently for about 40 minutes. (If you have any gherkins, eggs or carrots left, add them into the pot.)

●   Cut the string and remove before serving. They are very good eaten with buckwheat.

●   Jan, Krystyna's husband, says he likes the 'vegetarian' version, which is only carrots and gherkins rolled in a beef slice.

Restaurant Presence

It isn't cheap going to restaurants these days, so it's nasty when your night out, saved for or planned for, is ruined by a restaurateur who dislikes his trade, his food and you. Just because you haven't reserved a table doesn't mean you've committed a sin, which you have to expiate by being stuck near the kitchen door and by being ignored whenever you try to catch the waiter's eye.

British people are timid in restaurants. They get so embarrassed at making a scene that they put up with things that would not be tolerated elsewhere in the Common Market, where people are prepared to be far more common if the situation requires. My advice is as follows, and I speak from experience.

If the chairs are uncomfortable, get out as quickly as you can. Why should you pay for penance?

If the fish arrives still frozen in the middle and burnt on the outside, send it back. Don't be heroic! Turning the other cheek is not the same as being a doormat. Anyway, it isn't fair on the next timid diner who will suffer from your cowardice.

Trust your own common sense and eyesight. I once sent back an uncorked bottle of wine – Château Dregs. It disappeared and then the same bottle came back, this time with a sherry cork.

As you have to foot the bill, don't pay for insults. If the service is good, then virtue should be rewarded. If there is no service, don't pay a service charge without protest.

It is prudent to listen to the advice of the waiter, indeed it is only courteous, but never be bullied. It doesn't do either of you any good.

Now all this is pretty miserable stuff so I am going to mention a nice thing that happened to me.

I dropped in at the Dominican Priory at Leicester, when I took my place among the friars, which means 'brothers', and they were brothers to me. I had had a busy fortnight going from religious retreat to religious conference, and it was bliss sitting in a friendly kitchen regaled with a mug of strong tea and a slice of cake.

You can thank the Dominicans too, because Father Robert Sharp gave me a recipe for the best Bobotie of them all. When peace finally comes to South Africa, make a big one and celebrate. Father Robert's

Bobotie is an old traditional Afrikaner folk dish, originally based on superannuated goat or whatever meat was available at the time. Leftovers can be thrown in. 'The secret is in getting a balance between the flavour of curry and almonds, so that neither swamps the other on the palate,' he said. This version will serve 10 people. As Jewish cooking doesn't mix milk and meat, I think soya milk will be a good substitute for ordinary milk.

Father Robert's Bobotie

3–4lb (1.35–2kg) mince
½ pint (300ml) milk or coconut or soya milk
3 eggs, beaten
3 large slices of bread, including crusts, cubed
2–3 onions, chopped
1 whole head of celery, chopped
3 apples, peeled and chopped
1 handful raisins
3 cloves of garlic, crushed
2–3oz (50–75g) flaked almonds

5 rounded tablespoons curry powder
½ bottle almond essence
salt and pepper

Topping
4 eggs, beaten
¾ pint (425ml) milk or soya milk
salt and pepper

Decoration
sesame seeds
tomato slices

● Mix all the ingredients together in a large bowl (your hands are best for this job).

● Put into a buttered oven dish, cover and cook in a moderate oven, Gas 4/350°F/180°C for 45 minutes.

● Take out of the oven and mix; taste and adjust seasoning. Press the mixture down in the oven dish and level the surface. Beat the eggs and milk together, season and pour over the top. Bake at the same temperature for a further 30 minutes, until golden brown.

● Decorate at will with sesame seeds and tomato slices.

Vegetables and Salads

According to tradition, Adam and Eve ate only vegetables in the garden of Eden, and when the world is sorted out and redeemed, and the lion lies down with the lamb, they and we will all be herbivores and vegetarians together.

In the meantime, many of us have already reached this state for other reasons – such as queasiness, ideology, or cholesterol consciousness. Soya substitutes Quorn and tofu, and the pulses, can be shaped to look like meat. And there have always been vegetarian dishes that possess the heftiness carnivores crave – such as Imam Bayaldi from Turkey or Party Pie from the Mediterranean. Vegetables need not be side shows, they can be the centrepiece of a meal.

Being honest, I do find a vegetarian meal takes a bit more time, and a lot more imagination. But it can be done and it works out cheaper.

I used to get an aesthetic pleasure from looking at some cuts of meat. Liver, for example, had a strange iridescent colour. Now I get the same satisfaction from fingering lentils, and wonder at their curious greens, browns, greys and pinks. Also, a purple shiny aubergine is the most sensual of sights in a market.

'. . . and then the snake said he would be our agent and get our life story in a book.'

Revelling in Autumn

I have never really liked high summer. There is too much expectation around, too much waiting on the weather reports, and feeling aggrieved if the sun is there one moment and not the next. I prefer the first days of autumn, when you don't expect too much and can enjoy walks in a mac, and munch blackberries from the hedgerows.

And my prayers change with the seasons. I don't try so hard or expect so much. Instead of badgering God with all my hopes, I sit back comfortably in a pew, and start thinking of nothing in particular, just enjoying the light from the windows, and the quiet. I start to think of ways to make blackberry tart, and occasionally glance up to the eternal light and feel pleased it's there and I am here and we are together. The grateful feelings begin to shape themselves into thoughts and then into prayer, and unrushed and gently I drift into an autumn reverie.

Dear God, thank you for believing in me, though sometimes I don't believe in you that much. I can't give you a present like the souvenirs I brought back from holiday, because what can you give a being who has everything, but these thanksgivings are beginning to form in me, so please take them.

Thank you for my work. I complain about it quite a lot, and say I'm being overworked and all that, and I would like to have more free time, or enough money not to have to work. But it isn't really like that, and you and I know. I can't help thinking of all the people without work. It must take a lot of spiritual strength and guts to get your order and sense of worth from within.

I would also like to thank you for the cheap holiday I booked in a hurry. Though I said I really wanted to go to some place with a lot of culture and a bit of class, I did enjoy people enjoying themselves. I hope, Lord, you don't mind my bit of snootiness – anyway, you know I can't keep it up for long.

Sometimes I tell myself how nice it would be to live somewhere else, in a villa in Marbella for example, a long way from British winters. But it really would not suit me, and you probably put me where it's best. So thank you for autumn treats, harvest festivals, toasted crumpets, walking through the falling leaves, and the fireside and a cuppa as soon as I get home.

This Comforting Red Cabbage is a good autumn dish, and it goes well with vegetarian cutlets or sausages. My friend Claire in Newcastle makes wonderful red cabbage, and has given me many ideas.

Comforting Red Cabbage

3oz (75g) butter or margarine
1 onion, thinly sliced
1 small red cabbage, shredded
1 green pepper, deseeded and
  chopped
1 large dessert apple, peeled,
  cored and chopped
zest and juice of half a lemon

2 tablespoons redcurrant jelly
2 tablespoons seedless raisins
  (optional)
caraway seeds to taste
  (optional)
salt and freshly ground black
  pepper

● Melt the butter or margarine in a saucepan and fry the onion, cabbage and green pepper together until soft.

● Add the chopped apple, lemon zest and juice, redcurrant jelly, salt and pepper, and raisins and caraway seeds if you like.

● Cook gently for half an hour, adding a little water if the contents stick.

On the Yo-yo of Life

There are some very sad aspects of human nature, and it's prudent to admit them and confess them in oneself and others.

Why is it that someone else's newspaper is so much more interesting than your own? I suppose it's hard to admit you would love to read the *Daily Gossip* as you go to work in the morning, but feel you have to flaunt a 'heavy' to service your image. Such things count in the suburbs. But it's so much cheerier reading about what minor royals had for breakfast than about the pound going up and down like a yo-yo (and your savings with it).

Why is it that your neighbour feels he has to angle his paper so you can't read it as soon as he knows you want to? He is probably a good-hearted man who gives to Oxfam and is kind to dogs and such. But as soon as he knows you want his paper he becomes like a dog with a bone, and this is silly because both of you could read it quite comfortably.

Why does the lady in front of you at the Underground always want a season ticket, just as you are going to an interview for a job and your time and temper are precious? Can it just be an accident that she can't pay in cash but has to dither between a cheque or credit card? Is it always the same woman, and what has she against you?

Why don't you win on the Premium Bonds? Surely it's your turn at last? Why don't you win at anything? Is there a conspiracy against you?

Why do people at parties say they want to 'share their experiences' with you? You would like their shares in the stock market if you could get them, not shares in their unhappy past.

Well, I am going to share a recipe with you that Rabbi and Mrs Hugo Gryn shared with me. That's what we do with all good things – 'Spread them around, spread them around!' Rabbi Gryn tells me it comes from his mother, Bella, who lived in the Carpathian mountains. I have adapted it as all cooks do.

Cabbage Noodles

1 small white cabbage
1 medium onion, thinly sliced
2oz (50g) butter or margarine
1lb (450g) packet broad
  noodles broken into pieces

1 tablespoon oil
coarse salt and freshly ground
  black pepper

● Grate the cabbage finely. Place in a colander, sprinkle with salt, and leave for 1–2 hours. Rinse, drain and dry in teatowels, kitchen paper or salad spinner.

● Fry the onion and cabbage together gently in the butter or margarine until brown.

● Boil the noodles in salted water with a spoonful of oil added until tender. Drain and combine with the cabbage. Season well with salt and pepper.

● My own tip for cabbage is to cover it with a cheese sauce flavoured with mustard (English, not French).

Food Fit for a Fast

One of the great troubles in life is that the material world seems so solid, and the spiritual world so diaphanous, as slight as a chiffon scarf, and we wonder at ourselves for basing our lives on it, when it isn't 'real' like our refrigerators and vacuum cleaners and cars.

It also isn't guaranteed, like our building society accounts or our pension funds, if we are lucky enough to have them. And yet, when we are in trouble, when we are struck by illness or misfortune, it is that see-through world we have to rely on and, miracle of miracles, it has enough tensile strength to support our life. I think it is important every so often to reaffirm the existence and eminence of that spiritual world by an act which leaves its mark on the material world.

People fast for different reasons, and because one is valid it doesn't exclude the others. Some people fast because they want to 'afflict their souls'. The fasting is used as a self-punishment. I am wary about such a reason. It's best to go to a colleague or a priest or some other proper adviser before you start sitting in judgement over yourself, which is the prerogative of the Almighty.

Fasting means to me that I am not totally dependent on the 'real' world, that I can detach myself from it, and not be completely mastered by it. It certainly doesn't mean that I despise the material world – how could I write on cookery if I did! I am an in-between creature made of flesh and spirit, and I must do justice to both, because God created both.

It's difficult to give recipes for a fast period. If you make them too tasty they miss the point, but how do you make a palatable dish of dust and ashes? In the Holy Land, yesterday and today, most people, especially the poor, get their protein from dried beans and pulses. Esau, you may remember, sold his birthright for a pot of lentil stew, which seems excessive.

I think lentils are an appropriate dish for penance periods of the year. They probably figured prominently in the diet of the Holy Family and of the disciples.

Simple Savoury Lentils

1 packet (500g) brown or green
    lentils
1 large onion, chopped
some celery leaves
1 carrot, chopped
2 cloves of garlic, chopped
1 teaspoon ground cumin or
    curry powder
1 clove

1 dessertspoon vegetable oil
juice of half a lemon
salt and freshly ground black
    pepper

Garnish
fresh coriander or parsley,
    chopped
4–8 hardboiled eggs

● Soak the lentils for 1½ hours, then wash them in a sieve and cover them completely with water. Add the chopped onion, the celery leaves, chopped carrot, garlic, the cumin or curry powder and a whole clove, and simmer for 1–1½ hours, until the lentils are cooked.

● Drain, add salt, lots of freshly ground pepper, the oil and the lemon juice. Scatter over the coriander or parsley and serve with 1–2 hardboiled eggs per person. Mash the eggs into the hot, dressed lentils and eat with wholemeal or pitta bread.

● I don't add salt until the lentils are cooked because it tends to toughen them up. Packets of lentils vary – some are well washed while others, unfortunately, harbour little specs of grit or even small stones! Do pick them over yourself before washing. It isn't difficult and you get the knack quickly.

Packaging Holidays on a Platter

I first went on a package holiday many years ago when it was still unusual, exciting and also very cheap. As I remember we paid under £10 for four days and three nights – or was it the other way round? The departure and arrival times were so odd that I lost track of time and counted according to meals. We went south, but as it was midwinter that was an act of belief, not experience.

We set out when we ought to have been going to bed, and the departure hall was deserted, ghostly and ghastly. British airports hadn't yet got their act together, so the hall looked like a leftover from the Battle of Britain. There were no inflated buns at inflated prices – to be honest, there was nothing except some wooden benches.

When we arrived, wherever we went (I never got it clear, except that all in all it was good value) it was obvious that our resort had not reached completion. Streets started as Grand Boulevards but quickly descended into ways, then paths, then sheep tracks, and some of the hotels did not have roofs.

Our hotel was stunning. The foyer reminded me of the old Corner Houses of Maison Lyons and the Trocadero. After our strange night in the stratosphere, we looked grisly under the glittering lights of the plastic chandeliers and the neon loops which adorned the entrance. Still, it looked class, which is more than we did after our journey. Like bedraggled evacuees, we groped our way down, looking grey, to a breakfast of mood music, sticky buns and (more memories of Lyons) milk and a dash, with more of the former than the latter.

During our four nights and three days (or vice versa) they did us proud. All the meals had four courses, some minute and some mammoth, and more cutlery than I had ever contemplated. We also had little bottles of liqueurs made out of improbable but exotic ingredients. One lady said she would use them as scent. This did not seem unreasonable, considering their colour and smell.

Well, you don't get packages like that any more – except perhaps on adventure holidays. They belonged to days when Spain was still strange and Portugal off the map and a fiver would buy you full board.

This salad platter reminds me of that time.

Sort of Salade Niçoise

8oz (225g) new potatoes,
   cooked, peeled and diced
8oz (225g) cooked green beans
   (frozen or fresh)
8oz (225g) tomatoes, skinned
   and quartered
half a cucumber, sliced
5 spring onions
7oz (200g) tin of tuna, drained
   and flaked
4 or 5 anchovy fillets
black olives
chopped parsley

French dressing
⅔ cup mixed olive and
   sunflower oil
⅓ cup vinegar or lemon juice
1 teaspoon salt
¼ teaspoon pepper
1 teaspoon mustard powder
3 cloves of garlic
1 tablespoon sugar

● Arrange the potatoes, beans, tomatoes, and cucumber in concentric circles on a large round platter, leaving the centre empty.

● Arrange the spring onions around the circumference, and pile the tuna into the centre of the platter.

● Cut the anchovy fillets in half lengthways and lattice the salad, inserting the olives in the interstices. Scatter over the chopped parsley.

● Mix together all the ingredients for the French dressing; you can shake them together in a jar or use a processor or blender – either way is easy. Pour half a cup of the dressing over the salad (the quantities I have given make a whole cup – the rest will keep very well in the fridge). Serve.

Heaven

We were discussing heaven. A doctor said that patients who'd been thought medically dead and then brought back to life had described very similar experiences. They'd looked down on their bodies from above and then been drawn into a tunnel of singing light. They felt desolate when they were returned to life. He thought there was something in it. Another doctor said it was just lack of oxygen to the brain. What do I think? Well, like many secret materialists, I'd like faith to be a fact and spiritual things solid, but my own experience of heaven has come in a different way.

I first felt attracted to it as a child, when I climbed on to my parents' bed in the mornings, stumbled over some lines of poetry and was rewarded with a kiss and a cuddle. One morning I recited:

'My soul there is a country, far beyond the stars,' but my parents censored the next lines because they were far too Christian, and I continued with:

> 'If thou canst get but thither,
> there grows the flower of peace,
> the rose that cannot wither,
> thy fortress and thy ease.'

I forgot those lines in the years that followed. Heaven was a fairy tale, puberty and pimples were real. I remembered them again one summer when I went hitch-hiking with a fellow student – a shapely lass who carried a pepperpot to protect her honour. We travelled hopefully to Paris, then to Burgundy and then to Provence, discontented, though we didn't know why. None of these places was quite what it was cracked up to be, and finally neither were we to each other. So one day she packed her pepperpot and stood me up on a hot dusty road. And as I hitched alone I knew that sun and sex, though divine, aren't enough. I was in search of something that can't be found in this world – something which came from that country I'd learnt about in childhood.

Ruefully I remembered a student song:

> 'You'll never get to heaven in an old coupé
> for no coupé can go that way.'

You can't hitch to heaven because it's nowhere. I've since learnt from experience that it's somewhere, though off any map, and you don't have to wait till you're dead to enjoy it. If you direct your love towards it, and express that love in something done for heaven's sake, not your own, you can make heaven happen. You needn't hitch to it, you're in it, and the same light the near-dead describe begins in you.

Now this may seem high-flown, but try it out yourself and see. Do something unselfish for the sake of heaven. Because you're not a religious professional like me, you may find it easier to make heaven happen, because your good deed is more disinterested.

> 'If you get to heaven before I do
> just bore a hole and pull me through.'

And I'd do the same for you, mate. I'd do the same for you!

This recipe comes from a contemplative — Sister cook of Turvey Abbey. She calls it Copper Pennies. I call it Pennies from Heaven.

Pennies from Heaven

2lb (900g) carrots, sliced into rounds	¾ cup vinegar
	¼ cup sugar
2 medium onions, sliced into rings	1 teaspoon Worcestershire sauce
1 medium green pepper, cut into thin strips	1 teaspoon dry mustard
	½ teaspoon salt
1 tin of tomato soup	black pepper to taste

● Cook the carrots, onion rings and pepper, preferably by steaming them for 8–10 minutes.

● Drain and combine with the rest of the ingredients. Leave for 24 hours to marinate.

● I find you can at least double the amount of carrots, as long as the mixture is stirred frequently – and the sauce isn't quite so sweet. Sister cook's mother says that concentrated cream of tomato soup is best.

Fashioning Holiness

I teach at a Jewish seminary for training rabbis, and I am beginning to feel like Old Father Time as I watch the generations of students come and go. (Where does one buy a lanthorn and sickle?) But it is very diverting watching the changing fashions, sartorially and spiritually. When I was a student we were seen and not heard. Venerable and dignified rabbis brooded over folios of the *Talmud*, and uttered (they did not chat) profundities in an impressive goulash of German, English and Hebrew.

I still think in umlauts, and relapse into Central European 'pidgin' when I consider 'ze aye and ze zou' of Martin Buber (translation 'the I and the Thou').

Like my fellow student (no, this is not a mistake; after the war there were only two of us) I wore a charcoal grey suit and Marks & Spencer shirt, and tried to think clean thoughts in clean underwear.

The generations which followed had a straggly look. Their hair was

'I got the gear in Carnaby Street.'

longer and limper, and they weren't keen and eager but gazed at you dreamily with gentle cow-like eyes. If you didn't watch it they pressed a flower into your hand that was equally droopy, and what could you do with it? You couldn't just stand around with it — you looked too much like Oscar Wilde.

The lot that succeeded them were sort of Revivalists, Jewish-style. They wagged their heads over me, they tut-tutted because of me, and prayed at me. (Praying for me is fine, praying at me is low.) They overtrumped me with pieties, and looked rather like my grandpa bedecked with skullcaps, and fringes and other religious remembrances.

I got a shock and couldn't help thinking, 'Help, this is where I came in.' I was cheered as I found out during their training that their thoughts in fact were just as mine had been, two generations earlier.

When my students drop in on me to talk about life, I serve them this bean salad I learnt from my friend Pauline. It satisfies all ideologies and is good for students as it contains a lot of protein.

Pauline says, 'I put this together in a trice when, leaving my two luncheon guests chatting in the garden, I went to cut open my avocados and discovered them to be tired old wood merely masquerading as avocados.'

Desperation Beans

2 or 3 tins of different beans, and chickpeas if you have them
salad greens – watercress, lettuce, endive
French dressing
chopped fresh parsley (and any fresh herbs of your choice)
olives (optional)

● Mix together in a bowl the drained beans.

● Arrange the salad greens on a platter, and tip the assorted beans on top. Pour over the French dressing and sprinkle with the parsley and herbs, and olives if you are using them.

● I also add spring onions, and crushed garlic to the dressing. They give the beans body.

What a Tangled Web We Weave

I had put together all the bits and pieces for a dinner party I was having the next day and, as I went round the kitchen at midnight, tasting this and sipping that, I sang a psalm to myself, the one about sowing in tears and reaping in joy.

Well, I must have chosen the wrong psalm, because as I waited for my guests the next evening I idly glanced at my diary, saw the squiggle and suddenly the squiggle made sense. Instead of being a host to all my guests it was the other way round. I had agreed to be the guest of one of my guests. In other words instead of giving a dinner party I was supposed to be at someone else's.

Now there are all sorts of ways you can deal with that situation. You can try to cheat and bluff your way out. You can have a sudden attack of pseudo-somethingitis. You can try to shift the blame, and pretend everyone else was in the wrong. You can even try to convince yourself that this pretence is true. But the wages of these types of sin are guilt and self-contempt. As I've got older, little white lies seem tedious, ugly and confusing, and passing the buck is not religious.

My guest-host was Sister Mary of the Sisters of Sion. Yes, she said over the phone, she was expecting me. She had invited some special friends to meet me. Would she mind, I asked boldly, if I came with three other unexpected guests, whom I wanted her to meet? We would all be a half hour late. There was a pause and I told her my tale of woe. She was a true friend and, though shaken, said warmly that we should all come, and she would work a domestic miracle with the salmon. She did. She cased it in puff pastry and turned it into a sort of Salmon Wellington, which was filling and interesting. (The child in every adult loves things hidden in other things.)

There is a reward for confessing the truth – a release of energy and joy. It was the best dinner party I've been to for years. When I got home, I said another psalm, this time the one that starts, 'Surely, the Lord is good to Israel.' (I can't give you the number, as I never remember numbers, whether it's psalms, telephones, or credit cards.)

The dish opposite is a good extender, if your planned party grows out of all proportion. It's an exotic but filling salad, and you can add lots of vegetable bits.

Exotic Burghul Salad

1lb (450g) medium or fine burghul (crushed wheat)
1 teacup French dressing
1 cucumber, peeled and diced
4 tomatoes, chopped
1 bunch of spring onions, chopped
a handful of chopped fresh mint
a handful of chopped fresh parsley
3 cloves of garlic, crushed
2–3 red or green pimentos
any of the following: olives, courgettes, cooked and sliced, grated carrot, cooked peas
juice of 1 lemon (optional)
lemon balm or lemon thyme (optional)
salt and freshly ground black pepper

- Put the burghul in a bowl and pour a kettle of boiling water over it so that the burghul is well covered. Leave to soak for half an hour.

- Now press as much water out of it as you can with your hands (I use a clean teatowel and a colander).

- Add the French dressing, salt and pepper to taste, the diced cucumber, chopped tomatoes, spring onions, mint, parsley (and any fresh herbs from the garden), the garlic, and the pimentos if you have them. Serve with good fresh bread.

- The proportions and amounts need not be exact. You can also add olives, cooked courgettes, grated carrot or cooked peas – anything colourful that fits. If you like a lemony taste, which I do, add the juice of a lemon and some lemon balm or lemon thyme.

The burghul salad improves the longer you leave it in the fridge – overnight if you can. Served with smoked mackerel fillets, it makes a substantial, filling meal that is exotic and cheap.

It is always worth keeping a packet of cracked wheat in stock but make sure that it is fine or medium ground – smaller grains than pudding rice. The large stuff remains a bit too crunchy for my molars.

In the Gospel it says, 'The truth shall make you free.' This applies just as much to small things as to big ones – like a dinner-party that went wrong.

A Herbal Remedy for Healthy Living

Now I am getting 'old and grey and full of sleep' I am giving up discos in favour of gardening, where the hours are healthier. Part of this new passion comes from greed. I have also cut down on meat, and have to be more herby to give some taste to what is left. Dried herbs (apart from sage) are a pale shadow of the healthy, earthy herbs you get from the garden – the pungency evaporates with drying. In supermarkets, packets of fresh herbs are expensive, and only the better-known ones are available.

I find herbs easy to grow. I am not over-anxious about their fate and don't mollycoddle them. I just put a pot in the earth, scoop out a hole with an old tablespoon, make it feel at home with some water, and then don't interfere. To my surprise I now have real sage, rosemary, thyme (lemon and old-fashioned), chives and parsley. I look at them each day astonished, because I have always been a town person, and it surprises me that anything I plant can grow.

A keen grower told me to talk to my plants, and urge them on. Her own plants, she told me, responded to such back-chat. Everybody in Hampstead, she added, was having little chats with their chives and very self-consciously I tried to prattle to my potted plants but they didn't appear that interested, so I put on my transistor instead while I potted. This seemed to meet with a favourable response, because, as I've said, the blooms are bursting out all over.

Now a cauliflower is an everyday vegetable but it is exceptionally delicious as a salad, provided it is cooked *al dente*, so that the florets are not soggy but still have some bite in them.

Cauliflower Salad

1 large cauliflower	black olives
anchovy fillets	chopped chives

Dressing

3 tablespoons olive oil	2 cloves of garlic, crushed
1 tablespoon oil from the anchovies	1 teaspoon English mustard
	sugar
3 tablespoons sunflower oil	salt and freshly ground black pepper
3 tablespoons lemon juice	

● Put the florets of the cauliflower in fast-boiling water and cook until done but still crisp; drain immediately.

● Make the dressing by mixing all the ingredients together. Pour over the cauliflower in a bowl.

● Decorate the salad with thin slices of anchovy and olives. Strew with chives and chill in the refrigerator before serving.

Separate Lives

Some people live securely in their own lives, and some like me are constantly falling out of them into other people's. I picked up the phone and got a crossed line. 'The Reform Jews won't recognise her,' one woman says excitedly to another. 'Yes, they will,' I intervene helpfully. 'Who the hell are you?' she says angrily. 'Pardon,' I say hurriedly and put down the phone.

I had to take memorial prayers in a fancifully numbered new estate. I located the house, the door was open, and quickly distributed service books. The mourners goggled like goldfish, because they weren't Jewish mourners, just genial gentiles. 'Don't worry, padre,' they said, 'we're all part of the same world.'

Because they're part of the same world too, I cheerfully mix up 'Dallas' and 'Dynasty', much to my mother's disgust. I wonder, what if JR and Alexis eloped to Ambridge? And because I'm muddled and middle-aged, what if Mrs Dale and her Jim retired to Ramsay Street, pouring Pommie middle-class oil over the passionate waters of those Aussie pools. All soaps must share the same story, because their characters share the same nature − family rows over money or matrimony, the struggle between being mean or generous.

I learnt this lesson during the war when I was evacuated to twelve families in succession. Now my granny told me gentiles were different. They weren't warm hearted like us Jews. Cradled in a gentile lap, I decided this was codswallop. Some of my foster parents thought Jews were mean, but they'd never seen my granny give away her only winter coat. This was more codswallop. Experience, not theology, taught me that Christian love is not confined to Christians, and gentiles have Yiddish heart.

I then thought my foster parents were different from each other because they didn't come from the same class, but the same battle was fought in all their breasts − whether to treat me as a son or a skivvy, seeing the government only gave them 12/6d a week for my upkeep. As in the soaps, the scenery changed, but the plot didn't.

War blurs our common humanity, because it divides us into friend and foe, and underlines our differences. But in peacetime the task of religion is to help us refind our sameness. After all, if the lion can lie down with the lamb so can we, whether we live in Baghdad or Bexley-on-Sea. Why can't Crystal move in beside Del-boy Trotter into Nelson Mandela House? Hath not one Father created us – so why be snooty?

This 'Hunters' Dish' comes from my friends Molly and Henk in Holland, but it reminds me of my great great aunt, who came from White Russia, at the other end of the great European plain. This illustrates how good tastes leap over all frontiers. The only animal my great great aunt ever hunted was mice.

Frisian Hunters' Dish

2¼lb (1kg) peeled and boiled potatoes
3½oz (100g) butter or margarine
½ pint (300ml) milk
2–3 pinches ground nutmeg
7oz (200g) green or Savoy cabbage, shredded
12oz (350g) onions, sliced into rings
bay leaf
curry powder
1 tablespoon vinegar
9oz (250g) strong grated Cheddar
paprika
salt and pepper

● Mash the potatoes with 1½oz/40g of the butter, the milk, salt and pepper, and nutmeg, to taste.

● Cook the cabbage in a little water for a few minutes and drain.

● Fry the onion rings with the bay leaf in the remaining butter, and add the cabbage for the last couple of minutes. Stir in curry powder to taste and the vinegar (use the curry powder sparingly; you need only a suggestion of it).

● Put half the mashed potatoes in the bottom of a greased casserole dish, then the cabbage mixture and three-quarters of the grated cheese. Cover with the rest of the potatoes and top with the rest of the cheese and a sprinkling of paprika.

● Bake in a preheated Gas 4/350°F/180°C oven until a brown crust forms. This should take about 30 minutes.

Moving on in Life

A friend of mine rang me up and said she didn't want much out of life – terribly little, in fact – all she wanted was a bit of peace and security. I suppose that's what we all long for (or think we do), but life isn't like that. It can provide all sorts of goodies such as sun, sausages and smoked salmon, but not the things she wanted.

The first problem about life is that it won't stand still. Just as you think you know how to live, and have got it all worked out, you have to think about retirement and pension (if any) and what to do when you are past it. I get a bit bewildered, as in my religious organisation and hierarchy I had always thought of myself as a 'bright young thing', a 'new broom' and all the other nice things new generations pushing up to power call themselves. But at a conference I found myself standing beside the bar surrounded by a respectful circle of students, all of whom were egging me on to greater banalities.

Kindly but officiously they supervised my drinks. 'Yes, get him a *little* gin with *lots* of tonic!' I was no longer a rising young anything; they had turned me into a father-figure and a junior elder statesman. As it's better to accept the stream of life rather than fight it I accepted my role, and unloaded myself of all the platitudes that previously would have made me blush. My audience nodded approvingly, the more fatuous I became. I was doing what a middle-aged cleric should and, being conformist at heart, this relieved them.

Life involves lots of other things that are a far cry from peace and security. It involves choices and taking risks. When you choose one thing it's no use getting annoyed because you can't have the alternative too, and as for risks, well, living is a risk, and you can't be insured against Life.

But though life can't provide security, it can, as I said, provide some summer luxuries that are within anybody's grasp. Here is a cheap Party Pie from the Mediterranean. The quantities don't have to be exact and you can vary the vegetables according to your fancy or your pocket. It makes a lot!

Party Pie

2¼lb (1kg) aubergines, sliced
vegetable oil for frying
2¼lb (1kg) potatoes, peeled
  and sliced
2¼lb (1kg) courgettes, sliced
2¼lb (1kg) red or green
  peppers, sliced
2¼lb (1kg) onions

2 jars pasta sauce e.g. Ragú or
  Dolmio
dried herbs – thyme, oregano,
  marjoram, mint, basil
6 cloves of garlic, crushed
brown breadcrumbs
salt and freshly ground black
  pepper

●   Lay the aubergine slices on a plate, salt them and leave for at least 30 minutes. This rids them of their bitter juices. Rinse and pat dry with a teatowel or kitchen paper.

●   Now fry each lot of vegetables in turn until cooked, draining them on kitchen paper as they are taken out of the pan.

●   Layer the vegetables in a greased oven dish or casserole.

●   Turn out the pasta sauce into a bowl, stir in the herbs you want to use and as much of the garlic as you like. Season with salt and pepper, and pour it slowly over the vegetables in the dish so that it sinks down through all the layers. Sprinkle brown breadcrumbs over the top and drizzle a little more oil over them.

●   Bake in the oven at Gas 6/400°F/200°C for 20–30 minutes until bubbling and browned.

Puddings

Since the Second World War, sweets have become sinful like cigarettes. Low-calorie yoghurts and fromage frais have replaced the buttery, sugary, suet pastry of former times. An invisible skull and crossbones broods over that section of the menu. Sometimes it even surfaces in names, such as 'Death by Chocolate'. But every regime or diet that deals honestly with human beings has to comprehend the occasional blow-out and big bang – if only to prevent sweetness becoming obsessive.

Sweets do take the weight off some people's minds, even if they relocate it on their bottoms. Perhaps because sugar is sure instant energy, perhaps because it is a reminder of childhood. I know, when I was waiting for a hospital X-ray, from which I feared the worst, I ate two big bars of chocolate, and I celebrated the result (favourable) with a large pack of Halwah, made of sugar, nuts and sesame seed.

No! Neither low-calorie yoghurt nor a fromage frais would have done at all. Sorry!

Tranquil Hosts of a Dream

Occasionally you visit a place and feel that you have set foot in a dream. There is a French novel which describes this sort of situation exactly. It is called *Le Grand Meaulnes* by Alan Fournier and you can get it in English translation.

Well, it happened to me too. I had chosen a retreat house at random, and found myself heading to Leicestershire, a part of the world I hardly knew and which I associated only with the A1 and the M1 and hurried, hopeless meals at service stations.

The retreat house turned out to be an early Tudor country house, built on the ruins of an Augustinian monastery or priory. Apparently Thomas Cromwell had also felt the attraction because, on a list of monasteries meant for destruction, he had written 'Launde for myself'.

Well, he never got it! Before he could enjoy it he too was destroyed by the terrible state machine he had helped to set up. But it is not right to jeer or say, 'I told you so,' even after centuries have passed. Judgements belong to God, not to us.

The house is now run by a work group led by a kind and helpful Anglican canon and is open to all religious retreatants and others, whether Anglican or not. These are some of the things I liked about it and which will make me return.

The grounds of the house were inhabited by two donkeys who had their own special hay fund. Now, I am no Hebrew St Francis, but I have to admit that the presence of animals makes me sweeter. I like ducks, but I drool over donkeys!

I was very conscious in the chapel that this was a holy place, because I felt the force of all its past piety. Sometimes beneath the skin of modern England you can sense an older, sacred England of pilgrims and prayers. I did, here.

The food was delicious. Supper started with gazpacho and ended with chocolate profiteroles and red Leicester cheese. I got quite neurotic wondering what to nibble next. 'Oh, my paws and whiskers!' the March Hare exclaimed!

The house wasn't an institution, it was a home. I sat in the kitchen with Ruth, the kind canon's wife, and a retired missionary from

Mozambique (who was using her retirement to look after animals, humans, gardens and churches).

We spoke about piety, potatoes and puddings. After a hectic month in London it was just what I needed, and Ruth gave me a recipe, too. It is one of those easy-going ones that don't require quantities – so you can put away your metric conversion tables and measuring spoons and relax.

Crunchy, Creamy Apple Pudding

Serves as many as you like

sweetened apple purée	4 tablespoons golden syrup
whipped cream	2oz (50g) cornflakes
large lump of butter	

● In a dessert dish put a layer of sweetened apple purée (or stewed apple, but not too wet). Cover with a layer of whipped cream.

● Now for the gourmet touch: in a saucepan gently melt together a large lump of butter with the golden syrup. When it is all melted, stir in the cornflakes. Make sure they're coated and put them on top of the whipped cream. They will firm up into a sweet crunchy topping. I ate 4 portions of it so I should know.

The dream was over all too quickly, and I wrote this just before a committee meeting was about to take place in my office. Thank you, Launde!

Breeteesh & Englisch

My grandparents came from Russia. They were part of that struggling mass of poor people trying to get to America, the Golden Country – to escape poverty and persecution – who are commemorated on the Statue of Liberty. Well, my grandparents never made it. They only got as far as these islands, not even halfway.

My mother's father actually thought it was America – because a sailor told him so. It took him a few years to sort out where he was, and as my grandmother rarely ventured out of her kitchen she never did get it straight. They were after all only kids when they arrived – my grandpa, a boy fleeing call-up to Siberia, and Grandma, whom he met on the boat, a girl with a label round her neck, whose parents had been massacred in a pogrom.

Grandpa's nationality never got sorted out, and he ended up with a most peculiar passport. When the Second World War was declared, in 1939, they wanted to deport him to the Isle of Man, though he'd lived here over half a century. What nationality was he? He didn't know! Well, they said, he'd better find out. The Soviet Embassy finally issued him with a passport which had 'forbidden to return to the USSR' stamped in it, which sounds useless, but it saved Grandpa from the Isle of Man. He was bombed out three times in Stepney instead.

He and Grandma brought me up. They spoke to God in Hebrew, to each other in Yiddish, to me in Cockney, and they swore and made love in Russian.

I lived with them in a little row of houses in London's East End, without indoor loos or hot water. The Jews lived on one side of the street and the non-Jews, Irish Catholics, and Orange Protestants lived on the other. We didn't meet till the Second World War when the bombs blew us and our lives into each other, and after that we never sorted them out again. In the shelter we all sang together, as the bombs rained down, 'Rule Britannia', 'My Yiddisher Momma', 'There'll always be an England', 'Sweet Molly Malone' and 'We'll hang out the washing on the Siegfried Line', which was presumptuous and tempted fate. Sometimes in the shelters there were Shakespeare readings, which were new to me, as before I'd only heard him in Yiddish, and there had been a riot over *The Merchant*

'It sure is a funny world. He lives in Blackfriars and I live in Whitechapel.'

NERO

of Venice in its Yiddish version.

Now I was the second generation of my family born here and they all wanted me to be really British – which wasn't that difficult. After all, I already had a British Identity Card and later on a British passport to prove it. My Britishness was a registered fact proclaimed on innumerable forms and documents.

But I sensed what they didn't, that being British was not enough. It was too fuzzy and undefined. In these British Isles, there are after all four nationalities, some with non-English living languages like Irish, Welsh and Scottish Gaelic. There are also other just-alive languages, like Cornish and Manx. In addition, this goulash of nations contains great communities of a million or more Indians, East and West, together with lesser communities of Chinese, gypsies, Australians, Poles, Jews etc. The four main nationalities don't know much about each other, and know even less about the newer communities amongst them. I went to infant and junior schools, several grammar schools and two universities in England, but no one ever taught me Welsh literature, or about Scottish Kings, or how the Irish happened – though I read history. I wonder if it's the same with them about the English.

There are of course a few institutions that try to comprehend them all, or almost all, like the Crown. That's why I suppose my grandparents and parents were such royalists, collecting coronation mugs, mourning George V and George VI and identifying with both Elizabeths, mother and daughter. The monarchy was both British and definite.

But being third generation over here I felt moved to go one step further, to be not just British but English, which poses a problem – because there are no English passports or identity cards, and English flags and symbols rarely appear on flag poles and not at all on pound coins though Scottish, Welsh and Irish ones do. Becoming English isn't an official external act, but an unofficial inner attachment to a countryside rather than a country, to a literature, and a history – very much like the attachment of a Jew to her or his Judaism.

Now England is a complicated country to attach yourself to, as I found out when I was evacuated. It's a cat's cradle of class distinctions and nuances which confound the unwary. For example, if English people don't like you, they become more and more polite to you, so you never know where you are, and wonder if 'perfide Albion' is not French prejudice after all. Also they think 'nationalism' is everybody else's 'ism' and rather vulgar. Is this nationalism too? I still can't figure it out.

I only realised in fact how English I was when I was outside it. On a visit to Israel, I dreamt longingly of Edwardian terraced houses in the rain, and in Holland everyone laughed at my English mannered politeness – so unlike Dutch rude and healthy straightforwardness.

And then there are so many Englands. Which can an immigrant community identify with? There is the Cockney England of my childhood with its market humour, rhyming slang and jellied eel stalls. There is the England of county bazaars, and 'bring and buys', where you consume plum jam and cakes full of calories to prop up the church tower. There is the England of gentlemen's clubs in Pall Mall and St James, which serves Boodle's Fool and bread and butter pudding on mahogany tables in ecclesiastical whispers. There is the England of the Fat Lady in Blackpool and Brighton rock. There are so many of them, each a complete world with its own rules, unwritten but real, like the English constitution itself.

Over the years my inner naturalisation has happened. In English country churches my own religion links up with that on the monuments and epitaphs. And abroad I am nostalgic for Marmite on toast, Worcestershire sauce, Gentleman's Relish, and Boodle's Orange Fool.

This was the original recipe given me by the chef at Boodle's itself, in the heart of London's West End, in St James.

Boodle's Orange Fool

4 oranges	**1 tablespoon runny honey**
2 lemons	**sponge fingers**
1 pint (570ml) double cream	

● Grate the zest from one of the lemons and two of the oranges, then squeeze the juice from all the fruit.

● Whip together the zest, juice, cream and honey, until stiff.

● Line a straight-sided dish first with a piece of greaseproof or baking parchment in the bottom to avoid sticking and then with enough sponge fingers to line the bottom and sides.

● Fill with the cream mixture and chill for several hours until set. Turn out and decorate in any way you wish.

You can also serve this straight from the dish, in which case you won't need the greaseproof paper lining.

Old Habits Die Hard

I read a fascinating book by a Jew who'd converted to Islam. My enthusiasm upset my teacher – 'You should refute it, Lionel, not recommend it.' The rules of the religious cold war said so.

And I sinned again when I advised a member of my own reform synagogue to transfer to the orthodox, as she needed her religion clear-cut. My wardens were not amused.

The old rules were especially unjust to converts, who were acceptable if they converted to you, but traitors if they converted out. Take my friend Charlotte Klein, a traditional Berlin Jewess who died a Catholic nun and wrote against anti-Jewish prejudice in the Church, annoying everybody. She deserved thanks.

And after thirty years I still remember another lady, now dead – an elderly widow without children who spoke a strange Yiddish. She wanted to become Jewish but the old rules couldn't cope or do justice to her life experience. 'What are the differences between Judaism and Christianity?' we asked.

'Are there any?' she asked, puzzled. We stared back, more puzzled.

'Don't you see any differences between your childhood religion and your present one?'

'We light candles at different times,' she said. 'They do things differently in England.'

'But what happened to your childhood saints?'

'Funny,' she said, 'they haven't been around awhile.'

We discussed her history. A shy, pious girl from the Atlantic coast, terrified of the traffic, who'd come over here to work. Two equally terrified Jewish refugees took her in, an elderly woman and her son. When the old woman became ill, the girl took over the household and its religious duties, and when the woman died it seemed only natural to marry her son and continue the household on its pious course. Now the son had died, but would they bury her beside him in the cemetery?

'What religion do you think you are?' a colleague asked gently.

'I don't know,' she said, distressed. 'Does it matter, sir?'

The cold war seemed to rule again recently in another cemetery. In Auschwitz, Catholic nuns confronted Jewish protesters for the occupation of Europe's greatest graveyard. If only the holy spirit could get in, something new could happen. The nuns might say, 'We meant well – we didn't understand – we're sorry – we'll go,' and the protesters might reply, 'Don't go, sisters, the ghosts don't need us, their descendants do, let's work together to spare them more horror.'

But religious cold war ways have become habit, so they feel instinctive and right, and more confrontation creates more prejudice, and prejudice more murder. Religions, like people, can be prisoners of their past. Why not seek God in the *future*, in the *new* heaven and *new* earth He is working to create.

Apples are the fruit of contention in many folk tales. They are reputed to be the forbidden fruit in the garden of Eden and they are the golden apples of rivalry in Greek mythology. But in this recipe they have soothed all my guests, whatever their origin, or belief, and they are cheap.

Spiced Cox's Apples

4 Cox's Orange Pippins	1 cinnamon stick
¾ pint (425ml) apple juice	2 cardamom pods (optional)
3oz (75g) sugar	vanilla sugar or icing sugar to
4 cloves	dust

● Pare the skin off the apples with a potato peeler but leave the cores and the stems.

● In a saucepan bring to a simmer the apple juice, sugar and spices. When the sugar has dissolved and the juice is simmering, put the apples in to simmer for about 30 minutes, turning occasionally with tongs or a slotted spoon.

● Lift out the apples into a serving dish and continue to simmer the juice until it has reduced by half and is thick and syrupy. Pour over the apples and chill for at least 2 hours or overnight.

● Dust with vanilla sugar or icing sugar and serve.

Clerical Epicures and
Gourmet Ecumenists

I chatted to the minister at a church fête. Crazed by ecumenism, we
clergymen had all invited each other to our 'bring and buys and bun
fights' and we were all becoming paunchy for the sake of ecumenical
piety. 'You must have a slice – such a teeny slice – of this Devil's Food
Cake. I thought of you when I made it.'

Well, you can take that remark many ways, and I was careful not to
comment. Instead I munched my slice, liberally loaded with chocolate
butter cream. It contained, I thought, enough calories to cut out any
enjoyable meals for the rest of the week. These little sacrifices! But the
cake was good, and I decided not to be a hypocrite but make another
sacrifice, and eat another teeny slice before I left.

The minister and I chatted amicably as we munched and masticated
the goodies that were pressed on us. It is curious, but if you are
wearing a dog collar people always want to fatten you up, like a calf or
a goose in the Bible.

No, we didn't discuss meditation or contemplation, or the Bishop of
Durham, or why the cathedral roof fell in . . . or the position of
women, ecclesiastically viewed of course. We spoke instead of the
'trade union' matters which link priests, pastors, imams, and rabbis as
effectively as any members of committees on doctrine. We talked
about mother unions, harvest festivals and recommended rates of pay
for clergy (occasionally realistic) and car allowances.

We were curious about each other's jobs. 'What have you been
doing today?' I asked him. 'Checking on the chutneys and jams for the
competition,' he said. 'Tasted too many,' he added, 'feeling rather sick.
Still, it's all for the sake of the church, isn't it? What do you do, rabbi?
Study those great Talmuds and all that?'

'Not really,' I said, trying to match his honesty. 'Sit in my office, fill
in forms, and move files from the IN to the OUT tray, and back again.
That's life!'

I don't think either of us expected to do the things we were doing
when we were students at the seminary. I had a romantic idea of
eating grisly gruel and wearing out my kneecaps in damp prayers.

Instead I am called to serve God on committees and computers. But wherever you are there is the same battle between what is mean and what is generous, between integrity and falsehood. The same truths are tested in an office, on a pulpit or judging jams and chutneys at a church fête.

Here is a nice French flan my generous congregants made for me; unusual because you cook it upside-down. It is made of caramelised apples and is delicious with cream. You get the knack of it after one or two tries (the 'failures' are still delicious). It is called Tarte des Demoiselles Tatin after the Tatin sisters. Who they were, I do not know. Do you?

Tarte des Demoiselles Tatin

2lb (900g) apples
3oz (75g) butter
6oz (175g) sugar

Shortcrust Pastry
8oz (225g) flour
3oz (75g) butter
1 egg
pinch of salt
***or* a packet of frozen pastry**

● Make the pastry by rubbing together the flour (seasoned with a pinch of salt) and butter. Add the egg and a little water, knead into a ball and let the pastry rest for an hour.

● Core and peel the apples and cut them in thick slices. Butter a deep pie plate lavishly and spread half the sugar evenly over the bottom. Lay the apples on the sugar close to each other and sprinkle with the remaining sugar. Dot over the rest of the butter.

● Roll out the pastry and completely cover the apples with it. Cut two or three vents to let steam escape.

● Bake first on a low heat to caramelise the sugar, then turn up the heat to Gas 5/375°F/190°C for 35–40 minutes. Take the tart out of the oven and carefully turn it out on to a serving plate.

My Family of Friends

I haven't had much free time recently, so I've been out of touch with my friends. But in December when Christmas follows Chanukah, and festivals enfold us all, I make an effort and struggle through the rain and the crammed trains and uncertain buses to visit old friends.

For many town people (including me) our real family consists of friends. They're the ones who do our shopping when we're ill, or whom we dare to ring in the middle of the night without worrying whether we'll be told off.

They're the people we don't always have to be nice to, and whom we can quarrel with, because we know each other too well – and are secure enough to say sorry and forgive.

So when I go visiting I don't have to make excuses or account for my time. They don't try to make me feel guilty, which is a good test of true friendship. They just enjoy me (though this sounds immodest) as I am, not as I should be.

In Notting Hill Gate, I was very moved at the supper my friends provided. Many years ago, we all decided to sanctify our Sabbath in the old manner. Each of us brought a dish of food and in a chilly church hall we recreated the old family festival.

We said the service round our table and warmed each other up with affection and good wishes. All sorts of people joined in. A drug addict stumbled in from the street, and a real lord graced our table. Both became part of our DIY family.

As we sang the familiar songs and hymns in the candlelight, I felt a great wave of companionship streaming towards us from mutual friends who had left this life and whom we had remembered in our prayers.

That evening I pressed on through the rain, and dropped in on the Sisters of Sion in Bayswater. I have never had blood brothers or sisters, and such sisters and brothers are the closest I have come to possessing the real thing. They plied me with pastries and cake and coffee, and Sister Mary Camilleri gave me this recipe, which is a good swift sweet you can make for unexpected friends.

Sister Mary Camilleri's Swift Sweet

2oz (50g) butter or margarine	5oz (150g) desiccated coconut
2oz (50g) sugar (caster or brown)	1 tablespoon milk
2oz (50g) cornflakes, crushed	1 dessertspoon cocoa powder

● Melt together the butter or margarine and the sugar in a saucepan.

● Stir in the cornflakes, 2oz (50g) of the desiccated coconut, the milk and the cocoa powder. Cook for a minute, then cool and roll into balls. Roll in the remaining desiccated coconut. That's all! I rolled some in ground almonds, and they were good too.

That evening I finally ended up in the Czech Club near West Hampstead. Surrounded by pictures of Benes and Masaryk and the old Cardinal Beran, I felt I had fallen into a time warp, and had entered a café in Central Europe about fifty years ago before the horrors began. I looked at the list of the Czech airmen who had fallen in the war, and whispered a memorial prayer for them under my breath. I didn't know them, and they didn't know me, but they had died for my freedom. That is surely the supreme mark of friendship.

Quelling Quarrels with a Carrot

A lot of my time used to be spent on Canon Law. It wasn't easy as I got the backwash of broken marriages.

I used to hold the telephone a foot away as people sobbed their woes at me. The trouble was, nearly all of them were right!

One of the problems was that people said things without giving themselves a cooling-off time, and then it was too late to take them back. It's always wise to interpose something in the heat of a quarrel. A prayer is fine if you can do it, but lots of people feel out of sorts with God just when they need his presence most.

In the old days, before people knew the dangers, a cigarette was a standby. I suggest a carrot as a substitute. I know I always want to munch when I feel moody. Crunching a carrot in the middle of a quarrel would also reduce the high drama. 'How could you . . .' 'Don't you dare touch me . . .', and 'After all I've done for you . . .' and so on. A carrot would be a turn-off, wouldn't it, and not fattening like chocolates?

One couple I knew used to make up by assembling the sweets they liked as children. It certainly restored harmony in their household. They assembled luscious Knickerbocker Glories with different colours of jelly and cream. I suppose the things they quarrelled about were childish, so the solution had to be the same.

I learned a tip from them. When I feel angry, it helps if I make a simple sweet for myself and the family. Its delicious awfulness makes us all giggle. What about Quick Lemon.

Quick Lemon Pud

8oz (225g) lemon curd   crystallised lemon slices *or*
8oz (225g) fromage frais   chocolate flake
grated lemon zest

- Mix together the lemon curd and the fromage frais.
- Chill, and decorate with the lemon zest and the crystallised lemon slices or chocolate flake before serving.

Cakes and Counsel in Teacup Ministry

When I got my first job as a minister, I was nervous and asked around what it would be like and what would be expected of me. Oh, they said, a lot of it will be boring, and don't expect otherwise. You'll contact more committees than souls, and most of your time will be taken up with the building fund, the bazaar, and the Ladies' Guild. Their voices tailed off in a sigh.

So I arrived at my first post, apprehensive but snooty about building funds, bazaars, and Ladies' Guilds. But not for long. When the roof leaked the dribbles settled on me (having no respect for rabbis). Indeed, they ran icily down my back just as I was reading the sacred scrolls. I became quite earnest in my appeals for roofing. I gave a lovely sermon with the theme that just as God shelters mankind, so our roof should shelter others (I meant me). It was corny but popular, as the dribbles had settled on everyone, lay and cleric alike, and ruined an assortment of bowlers, berets, and flowered Ascots.

I also got addicted to the tombola at the bazaar. There was a terrible electric toaster which always got thrown back in. I only learnt its nasty nature after I won it, rejoiced, plugged it in, and fused the lights. Oh, it always does that, they said smugly, after I told them. I did not throw it in again but virtuously got it repaired. I have learnt since that it has reverted to its hostile habits.

My poor patronised Ladies' Guild in fact kept the congregation together in everything that mattered. You don't have to be ordained to be a minister. There are all sorts of ministries, some recognised, some not, some paid, some not, but none the less efficient for being voluntary.

For example, there is the ministry of the teacup, the most important of all in a big city, where people can be holed up in homes or bedsits by babies, age, domestic duties or agoraphobia. My Ladies' Guild were a conscientious lot, and with the tea they gave away cakes and counsel far better than mine, because it was more realistic and direct.

After sizing me up, they ministered to me, too. They didn't just darn my shroud and brush my robes. They also told me how to wash a body for burial, how to go about finding lost spouses, and not to waste time sulking over the cosmos when somebody needed to be seen to.

Some of their meetings were uproarious, and I wished I could be present to hear the jokes they told each other, but there they drew the line – they had ministered to the minister enough.

This recipe would have appealed to them. It comes from a Gemma who interviewed me for RTE. She sat through my cookery demonstration and was complimentary about my potato cakes (Jewish, not Irish style). I think this recipe she gave me is as good, and better than anything I cook up. I have always liked Irish bread, but I never thought of turning it into frozen cream.

Brown Bread Ice Cream

3oz (75g) wholemeal breadcrumbs – the nuttier the better
3oz (75g) brown sugar

½ pint (300ml) whipping cream
1–2oz (25–50g) caster sugar

● Combine the breadcrumbs and brown sugar and spread them out on a baking tray. Put the tray in the oven at Gas 6/400°F/200°C for 10–15 minutes until the crumbs are browned; stir the outside crumbs to the centre halfway through. The idea is to melt the sugar so that it oozes into the breadcrumbs. You could do this under the grill but it burns easily. Leave the mixture to cool – it will harden.

● Crush with a rolling pin or whizz in a processor until fairly fine but not powdered.

● Whip the cream until thick, fold in the caster sugar and then the breadcrumb mixture.

● Freeze (you don't have to do any stirring).

● Serve with brandy poured on each portion. It's delicious and tastes like an expensive praline ice cream. You can eat it straight from the freezer.

Singing Nuns are
Now Less Frequent

I recommend retreat houses for happy budget holidays – and here's some very personal advice.

They vary a lot. Most are chatty, chintzy and modern. A few still have high brass bedsteads with pre-war wardrobes (wonderful for treasure hunts), and the liturgy, like chewing gum, stretches out forever. Actually, I like these best. You don't get separate bathrooms, and in England no bidets – retreatants aren't expected to require them.

Your fellow retreatants are a mixed lot, but most are middle aged and middle class – so they pass plates, don't tch-tch-tch at you with their Walkmans or engage you on abortion, birth control, gay rights, the second sex, or any sex, over breakfast. But they can burn the toast. There's often a bar, where someone will listen to your woes even when sober. Singing nuns with guitars are now less frequent here than in France.

But of course you're not going on a retreat for bidets and bars, but for religious experience – well, here's some frank advice on that, too. Firstly – rejoice! because it isn't that rare. If it were, religion would have packed up long ago. After all, people don't like talking to themselves – they want feedback. In fact, I don't see how you can avoid religious experience. You're released from routine and the rat race. You awake to birdsong and the aroma of smoked haddock, and nobody pushes you around. If you sit in the silent chapel each night before you go to bed, some inner release is bound to happen. I'm sure of it.

Second tip. When it does, don't get high on it. It isn't an instant cure-all. Two weeks ago I went on a mini retreat and returned to London in a golden glow. A few hours later I had a ferocious row with a friend over what to wear at a dinner party. At table we sat tight-lipped, talking not to, but through each other, to the suppressed fury of my hosts, who won't ask me again.

Now my religious experience on that retreat was real enough. What happened was that a bit of me had gone ahead of the rest of me, which

would take a year, or a lifetime, to catch up. In the meantime, I and my friends are in for a rocky ride. Be warned!

Third tip. Don't worry about it, because the loveliest experience of all – connoisseurs of religion and life all agree – isn't first raptures but making it up after a row. You don't need a chapel or retreat house for that. It's available any time, anywhere, and in religion it's called repentance.

I have now risen in the spiritual scale. I am not only a retreatant to a retreat house, I am also a governor of one – Ammerdown near Bath. I am therefore in a good position to taste and cadge bits from the kitchen and recipes. This quick syllabub was given me by June Mathews, the wife of the director, the Reverend Melvyn Mathews. I ate a pot of it while reading his book *The Hidden Journey*.

June's Quick Syllabub

Serves 8

½ pint (300ml) double cream	1 large tin of condensed milk juice and rind of 3 lemons

- Whisk up the cream until thick. Pour in the condensed milk and whisk further until thoroughly mixed. Stir in the lemon juice and rind, and then chill in the refrigerator.

- Serve with shortbread biscuits.

It Wasn't Jam!

It's a strange business giving sermons or religious radio talks. Like paying with cheques or credit cards. You can't just give them, you have to back them. Sooner or later, God presents your wise words for payment, and that's when you find out how much they're worth.

Take last week, when I gave out a lot of good advice about how to be happy in hospital. Well, before the week was out, I was back in one again, mulling over my own advice. I was on my way to a religious conference in Holland, and I'd treated myself to a break en route. I'd had a hard year, and I sat on a bench in the autumn sun beside a beautiful canal. I opened my mouth for a bite of even more beautiful Belgian chocolate. Then I opened my eyes, and wondered. Why was my face covered with jam? Well, it wasn't jam, and I wasn't any longer on a bench, but stretched out in an ambulance. The nurses were gentle and matter of fact. I'd blacked out, convulsed and collapsed and I'd bitten my tongue badly. No, no one had picked up my chocolate.

In hospital, they put me to bed and left me fretful and fed up. God had presented my words for payment, and I could only say the same silly things as everybody else. 'Why me? Why now? It's not fair!'

Indeed, life isn't fair, I thought indignantly. We don't own the freehold of it or even the lease. We haven't got rights like mortgagees. We're no more secure than tenants at will in this world. We've got no more security than that, however much knee work we put in. Sooner or later we say goodbye to everything we've been given – our brains, body, the lot – gracefully or with a growl, it makes no difference.

I felt so sorry for myself, that a tear trickled down my cheek. 'What do I do?' I whispered. 'You could do worse than take the same advice you hand out to others in your sermons and books,' said that old familiar voice inside me. 'Things do work out, Lionel, if you trust. That's what religion's really about. That's the name of the game.'

My pride made me follow my own advice. I tried to accept my situation and relax into it. I was tired, and as I looked round the ward it seemed white and peaceful and the other patients a pleasant and supportive lot. A wave of contentment welled up in me, from where I don't know, or why. And when I began to pray, what came out astonished me. It was a prayer of thanksgiving, though thanks for what, God alone knows, a little epilepsy, maybe! I was even inspired to tell the bods in the beds nearby one of my dreadful jokes in my even more dreadful Dutch.

'What do sea monsters feed on?' I asked brightly. *'Wat eten zee monsteren op?'*

'Vel wat?' said the other patients patiently.

'Fish and ships,' I said triumphantly. *'Vis en pommes frites,'* I explained helpfully.

'Pommes frites!'

They glanced at each other and then at the docket fixed to my papers for a brain scan. I was crestfallen. But they were more sympathetic than ever after that, and they gave me lots of lovely white chocolates, much better than the bar I'd lost. 'Yes, if you trust, things often work out,' I thought. 'God doesn't cheat, even on the chocolates, but they don't work out, I admit, in any way you ever expect or want. That's life – sorry!'

This recipe was given to me by Mrs Eileen Carey in the foyer of the BBC. She was just jetting off to a fraught ecumenical conference, and it was nice of her to remember me. It's a very suitable coda to this tale, as it's a pudding made of chocolate Mars Bars (which are a passion of mine, in classical or frozen ice-cream form).

Mrs Carey's Confection

5 standard Mars Bars	**1 pint (570fl oz) double cream**
1 packet (7–8oz/200g) Boudoir biscuits	**grated chocolate to decorate**

● Freeze the Mars Bars in a plastic bag until they are firm, then smash them with a rolling pin or wooden mallet. If you prefer your chocolate softer, leave it a little.

● Crumble the biscuits and whip the cream until thick.

● In individual wine glasses layer the crumbled biscuit, the crushed Mars Bars and the cream, finishing with the cream. Decorate with grated chocolate.

Baking

When I retire I shall bake. Not because I am any good at it, and the supermarket stuff will be cheaper and better. I shall bake for the sake of the smell. What incense is to churches, so hot pastry and dough are to kitchens.

I too have a dream. I see myself in a rustic stripped-pine kitchen, looking wise in the ways of nature, stirring strange ingredients I have gathered from hedgerows into curious breads and conserves according to recipes collected from grannies in country cottages, all the while dispensing rural wisdom to entranced tourists, who, as they munch, say 'My, my, Rabbi!' in wonder.

Well, that's the theory of it. In practice I use bought puff pastry and make my shortcrust in my processor. I also like those mixes where you feel virtuous as you add an egg. For very fancy stuff, God created supermarkets!

But I have learned, laboriously over the years, how to make simple soda bread and some simple shortcuts with cakes. If you are not the world's most wonderful pâtissier, read on. If you are, you can just read the spiritual introductions and feel snooty and superior.

How I Learned to Face Up to my Fear of Hospices

I want to thank the sisters, staff and chaplain of St Joseph's Hospice in Mare Street, Hackney, London. I'd had a heavy week, and my outlook was not made more sunny with the knowledge that my hospital wanted to insert a catheter into one of my arteries. I had not the slightest idea what a catheter looked like – whether it was like spun sugar or a length of old rope – but arteries and veins always make me feel nauseous. It's better to think about nice things instead.

So a visit to a hospice was not my idea of an outing. I wondered whether to call it off. Now, if I had called it off, I would have felt much worse. It's only through facing fears that they are dispelled – that's the only way our anxieties turn inside out, and we find that what we are afraid of is our own fear.

The hospice is a nice place – no, it's more than that, it's a loving, caring place. The patients are not there to be cured but healed, and both their body and soul aches are taken seriously and treated. Some, though, are both cured and healed, for our souls and bodies still surprise us.

Some smoke. One offered me a glass of wine. I met an old acquaintance. There was a tea-party in a garden (in the middle of Hackney!), and I had a very nice time.

Now, babies come crying into the world, and most people feel wistful when they have to leave it. There are, after all, so many loose ends in a human life, but the presence of supportive love makes all the difference.

So when my times comes I shall make for Mare Street if they will let me in. Although I hope it will be years, even decades yet, I would still like to be prepared and have something to look forward to.

You can't, of course, live on love alone (and your life in a hospice is real living), so food is important, as are friends and efficient pain control. The Sisters at the hospice told me how Marks & Spencer helps them with gifts. It's nice to pass on good news.

One of the things I shall look forward to is the good brown bread I ate there. Home-made bread is a great comforter and reassurer. I have never been good at making it, so Sister Ann's simple recipe from the hospice is helpful.

Sister Ann's Irish Soda Bread

8oz (225g) self-raising flour	1 teaspoon salt
8oz (225g) wholemeal flour	12fl oz (350ml) soured milk or
1 teaspoon bicarbonate of soda	butter milk

● Mix together all the dry ingredients and, using a wooden spoon, stir in the milk – the mixture should be moist but not too wet.

● Turn the dough on to a floured board, knead lightly and form into a round loaf.

● Place on a greased baking tray, and bake in a preheated oven, Gas 8/450°F/230°C for 15 minutes. Lower the temperature to Gas 5 or 6/375°–400°F/190°–200°C and bake for a further 20 minutes. Leave to cool on a trivet so that the bottom of the loaf does not become soggy.

The Royal Gentleman

I went to tea with my friend. She poured tea calmly from her old silver teapot, passed me my cinnamon toast, and told me she only had a year to live. How should she use her time?

'Write a book on English spirituality,' I said. She looked at me enquiringly but I couldn't give her the reason. She'd have thought I was over the top, but she was the finest example of spirituality I knew. She was a lady.

She died as she completed it, anxious about washing her own smalls, and putting her papers in order to spare her family and friends the trouble.

Once, when we were discussing her book, she said, 'Lionel, which English person helped you most, spiritually?' And though I hadn't thought of him for years, to her surprise and mine I suddenly named the old king, George VI.

At school we all got mugs to celebrate his coronation. It was a worrying time for a small Jewish lad in London's East End. In Germany, old Jews like my grandparents were forced to wash pavements, my cousins died in Spain fighting Fascism, and closer to home, when Mosley tried to march through the East End my father landed in hospital and my grandfather in the police station.

My parents said the new king was a decent chap but of course he had no chance against such gangsters. He was knock-kneed, and he stammered. He dreaded public appearances and people said he wasn't that bright.

But he was a gentleman. So during the war we trusted him because we knew he'd never walk out on us, even if we were invaded and we lost. And he would never collaborate with evil, as smarter and cleverer people did, because it isn't a thing gentlemen do.

Now, in modern times official saints, visionaries and mystics have been in short supply over here. We even import our evangelists from America. Our spiritual speciality has been Ladies and Gentlemen.

I mean the real thing, of course. You don't become a gentleman by wearing a blazer with a set of club buttons, or a lady by wearing pastel twinset and pearls. It isn't dining with 'in' people at 'in' restaurants. As Grandpa said, 'A gentleman isn't a gentleman because he comes out of a door that says so.'

It means passing plates at parties and being polite to people you don't take to. It means keeping your word and appointments and doing your duty without making a song and dance about it. It means not saying or doing things you'd like to, because ladies and gentlemen don't do them. It means putting your papers in order before you die, to spare your family and friends the trouble.

It doesn't sound exciting. It's not spiritual cake, just boring old bread. But you can survive on your dull, daily bread – you don't need fancy cake. We found that out when it was a matter of life and death, when there was a war on.

Now here is a recipe for daily bread that is not dull. In fact, I would happily eat half a loaf without anything on it. I only wish I could bake some for my friend, but she has moved on – alas!

Richard's Daily Bread

2lb (900g) wholemeal bread flour
3oz (75g) cracked wheat or bran
½oz (10g) salt
2 tablespoons black treacle
1¼ pints (720ml) warm water
1oz (25g) dried yeast

- Mix the dry ingredients in a large bowl.

- Stir the treacle into ¼ pint (150ml) of the warm water and sprinkle the yeast on the top. Put in a warm place for 7–10 minutes, then stir in the rest of the warm water.

- Add the yeast mixture to the flour bowl and stir well to form a sticky dough.

- Divide the dough between 4 × 1lb (450g) well-oiled tins. Dampen your hands and press the mixture down into the tins. Leave to rise in a warm place for about 40 minutes.

- Bake at Gas 6/400°F/200°C for 30 minutes. Take out of the tins and bake for a further 5 minutes for nice, crisp loaves.

Have We Got Problems?

'Rabbi, give us some thoughts with social significance!'

I froze because I don't know how to solve the Palestinian problem and I've no good advice to give to Mr Gorbachev that he hasn't had already, and I don't think Catholics or Protestants in Ulster would welcome a rabbi preaching at them.

But, diffidently, here are some suggestions for social and spiritual services, which I know are needed, and which nobody has got round to yet.

Is there any organisation which can help small businesspeople when they are going through a rough time? They don't only need a loan (who doesn't?) but an accountant, too, and some sympathetic counselling to relieve the strain that often takes its toll on their marriages.

Who helps people in mixed-faith marriages to sort things out . . . angry relations, problems of children's education, celebrations, etc? Such marriages are common now, and the couples and their problems get passed from one faith to another, no one knowing what to do with them.

Are there chaplains to soccer societies and football clubs? Could the more muscular ones transfer their attention to our yobbos? People are often violent when violence has been done to them.

Is there any religious order to look after tourists who stream like lemmings into the Costas? They don't only suffer from sunburn, but also from loneliness, booze and shattered romance. A friar or sister, propped up beside the hotel bar, might be just what they need. I know some of the tour operators have chaplains for the oldies, but what about young chaplains for the youngies? They suffer much more from 'life' and some eternal life would help them to get this one in perspective. The only group I've met who've put their skates on is the Sally Army! Any others with a vocation for common, common market types on vacation?

Who helps students and novices when they have left their seminars or religious orders – sometimes after studying and serving for many years? They need as much support and affection as those who stayed in – more, perhaps, because they don't know where they are. It's a test of caring for all faiths. There's lots of nice things said when you enter, but not much, if anything, when you leave.

It's also tough if you've fallen through a hole in the social system. There was a nice chap who'd been sent home from a psychiatric hospital. But 'home' had collapsed while he was away. He was fit physically but he needed friends who could be his family. Are there families for people like him?

I've been to a lot of religious conferences. Religion must be relevant to the needs of the world, we tell each other. But the world isn't far away – it's on our doorstep.

And here's something to give you strength to face them, so it's a real, if modest, contribution to social significance. It was given me by a friend whom I meet at religious conferences in Germany. She was brought up in South America, and this cake was part of her early life.

Edith's South American Cuca Cake

8oz (225g) butter
6oz (175g) sugar
3 large or 4 medium eggs
8oz (225g) flour

1½ teaspoons baking powder
ripe bananas
ground cinnamon

● Beat together the butter and sugar, then beat in one whole egg at a time. Stir in the flour with the baking powder.

● Grease a shallow baking pan, spoon in the dough and cover it with a thick layer of sliced ripe bananas. Sprinkle with cinnamon (and sugar if you like).

● Bake in the oven, preheated to Gas 4/350°F/180°C for 35–40 minutes.

● When it is cooked, cut it into little squares.

Old Time Office

The atmosphere in offices has changed so much that it is no longer recognisable to an old-timer. Technology has made the difference. Offices used to be busy, bustling places, alive with all sorts of noises. Typewriters clacked and at the end of each line a bell rang. Mechanical, non-electric adding machines cranked and choked as they tried to add 1/9d to 2½ guineas. I could do that once in my head, but I don't think I can any more.

Most oldies are in the same boat. It was all right subtracting 1½d from 2¼d if you had to do it constantly in shops and trains. But if you are out of practice, reach for your solar-powered calculator. Bosses also didn't whisper into mikes, they bawled out letters to prim secretaries who scratched little thick and thin lines over their notepads.

My favourite machine was a copier. It didn't work with photocopies, but with jelly, purple ink, and queer crinkly paper. It fascinated me, and I came home every day looking as if I'd been dipped in blackcurrant jam.

There was also the fascination of a non-automatic telephone exchange. You connected plugs from one hole to another. When there were a lot of calls, plugs crossed each other like bowlines or lovers' knots, and it was a hardy telephonist who didn't have hysterics. Plugs were popped into wrong holes, and the sparks flew, sometimes between the speakers who were connected to unwanted conversations. You picked up the telephone, and heard things your best friends didn't dare tell you.

There was a lot of talk and chatter, with office boys being cheeky to secretaries, and a Cockney tea lady climbing around with a pail of stewed tea, thick with tannin and laced with condensed milk. I think this taste was a leftover from the war. That's how the fire watchers liked it. It was a meal as well as a drink. You've had a recipe for a banana cake. Here is a recipe for a banana bread. It comes from South Africa, not Brazil, and you eat it cut in slices and buttered.

Banana Bread

8oz (225g) plain flour
a pinch of salt
3 teaspoons baking powder
2oz (50g) soft margarine
2 soft ripe bananas

2oz (50g) caster sugar
1 beaten egg
½ teaspoon cinnamon
milk

● Sieve together the flour, salt and baking powder, and rub in the margarine.

● Mash the bananas with the sugar, beaten egg and cinnamon, and then mix this into the flour and margarine. Add enough milk to make a sticky mixture.

● Spoon into a small greased and floured loaf tin, and bake for 45 minutes in a preheated oven, Gas 4/350°F/180°C, until brown and risen.

French Leave!

A friend of mine asks me if I would like to borrow her holiday home in Normandy. Wouldn't I just! I shoot off towards it like a stone from a catapult, lured by cows, Camembert, and Calvados. I then remember that Camembert is out (cholesterol) and so is Calvados (sugar) but tell myself 'abroad is different', which is not logical, but feels as if it is.

I enjoy the Channel ferry, because it not only takes me forward to France, it also takes me back in time. I marvel how little ferries have changed. There are the same shaggy hikers, bent double under the same loaded rucksacks. There are the same students singing folk songs while everyone else wants to sleep. There are the same sprawling figures, hogging the same chairs, and the same debris littering the corridors round the cafeteria. *Plus ça change!* I say to myself self-consciously, and wonder if I've got the grammar right.

But some things have changed. There is no first-class forward, no abyss separating the first class goats from the second class shaggy sheep described above. The class struggle has ended on the Channel as well as in Eastern Europe.

In Normandy I rush to a supermarket to fill the larder. I am rocked — there are no baked beans. What, no baked beans! I cannot believe it, and I hunt round the bottles and tins of haricots again. But it's true. The French really are different, I am truly abroad.

The curry powder is also expensive and canary colour. I ask a French housewife, who informs me that French curry is a matter of lightly flavoured spiced cream. I remember the French never really knew India — only Pondicherry.

Prices are higher, but quality is better, and I have to rethink my menus, which sounds grander than the reality. Artichokes are cheap, and avocados are sold by the kilo, which is bliss, as I consume them as hors d'oeuvres, and also as desserts, mashed with cream, sugar and lemon juice.

The wine situation also puzzles me. Cheap wine is really cheap — three bottles with nice labels for under eighteen francs — less than £2. On the other hand, expensive wines are, well, expensive, and as much out of my range in France as in England. I also buy a lot of cheap cider.

It looks cloudy and authentic, and when opened it is, with the flavour of farms and orchards.

Cheeses are cheap enough, also, with nice farmyardy smells and crusts. If I'm going to collapse for a Camembert, I might as well include a Livarot as well, which I prefer. I shall return to my soya and tofu 'cheese' when I'm back home in Britain.

It is surprisingly easy in France to pack a picnic – the pâtés, cheeses and nibbles are so abundant and various. The French do not sit on grass or make a virtue out of eating rough. They unfold tables and chairs, provide napkins and a *poubelle* per person for the inevitable litter.

For those interested in pilgrimages, I suggest one route scarcely known in England, to the abbeys lining the lower Seine – St Wandrille, Jumièges, etc. The ruins are magnificent, and the monks have come back. Piety and pâté make a lovely combination.

A French lady married to a Scotsman gave me this recipe for the most melting of cakes, rather like a rich mousse.

Chocolate Cake

4oz (110g) unsalted butter	4oz (110g) caster sugar
4oz (110g) dark chocolate, such as Bournville	3 flat tablespoons flour
	3 eggs, separated

• In a double boiler or over a *very* low heat, melt together the butter, chocolate and sugar.

• When amalgamated, take off the heat and add the flour and egg yolks.

• Beat the egg whites until stiff and fold in.

• Pour into a buttered 6–7-inch cake tin and bake at Gas 4/ 350°F/180°C for 45 minutes or until a sharp, pointed knife comes out of the centre clean and dry.

• Scatter grated chocolate or icing sugar over the top, if you like.

Bon appétit!

Poor, Tired Shopper

The following is meant for those of you who aren't particularly religious, who go to places of worship only for weddings and funerals.

You've come to town to do your Christmas shopping, which isn't easy when there's a recession on. Everybody's hunting through the bargain basements for pressies that look a lot but don't cost it. A big woman's pushed past you to that superglow mutant turtle you wanted and an old gent has prodded you with his umbrella and then trodden on your toe. He looked so saintly, too.

You're worn out before you've begun, so you decide to treat yourself to a slice of fruit cake and a cuppa. But on the fourth floor of the department store there's a conga line of customers snaking round the self-service, so you give up. Where can you park your poor, tired tootsies? A carol comes over the tannoy and it gives you an idea. Why not park them in some nice warm church – if you can find one?

Which is not so easy. Sure, there are loads of them around, but they're all locked. Now don't get paranoid. The clergy haven't got anything against you. It's the insurance that's the problem. Not everyone who drops into empty churches has such a nice nature as you. Some people nick things, even the poor-box by the door. But if you seek you'll find. I had the same problem, but eventually I found two convenient chapels not far from the department stores – one filled with flowers where they gave me a free lunch, and the chapel in Middlesex Hospital, which glows with golden mosaics. You can't nick mosaics without nicking the walls that go with them.

OK, when you've found one, what do you do in it? It's awfully empty, and there's no service on to tell you when to stand up, sit down or wave your hymn book in the air. It's also very silent, and what do you do with that? After all, you're only an ordinary tired shopper with a downtrodden toe, you're not into marvels, miracles or visions.

Well, honestly, I'm not either, but here's some practical advice from a religious professional, which may help.

First, find a pew with a cushion beside a radiator and warm your toe. Don't gabble all your sins at God – they aren't original and he's heard them all before. Why make both of you miserable? You don't have to do anything – just be. It takes two to tango in divinity as well as on a dance floor, so relax, be patient and let God find you – let him make things happen.

Sometimes he finds you without words. The traffic noises fade away and a wave of peace floods through you. You even hope the kid who gets the superglow turtle, your turtle – enjoys it. Sometimes you get into a kind of conversation with God. No, you're not going crazy – it happens to lots of people, including me. If the inner voice makes you kinder and more compassionate, go along with it – it's the real thing. Your prayers might not change the world but they'll certainly change you.

Now, being a shopper, you wonder if it's any use asking God for things. Sure, why not! Provided you realise he can say no. In practice my prayers don't make my problems disappear, but they do give me courage to face them. They don't stop me having rows with my nearest and dearest, but they do help me to make up afterwards. They've never made me rich but they make me feel rich, because I can give my bar of chocolate to the down-and-out at the door.

That's enough serious stuff for a cookbook. Here's a joke about a shopper – a little naughty but nice, and I hope it cheers you up as you go back to fight the good fight in the bargain basement.

A lady passes a shop with clocks in the window. She goes in and says to the old man behind the counter, 'I'd like to buy a watch. Which do you recommend?' 'I know nothing about watches,' he says, 'I'm not a watch-maker.' 'Then what are you?' she asks tartly. 'I'm a Jewish ritual circumciser,' he says. 'Then why have you got all those watches and clocks in the window?' says the lady indignantly. 'Madam,' replies the old man wearily, 'what should I put in the window?'

To return to that aforementioned slice of fruit cake that shoppers long for. Why not make it yourself and take it along with a thermos of tea? Then you can sit outside Selfridges, Harrods or Marks & Spencer, quaffing and chuckling happily to yourself.

The following fruit cake recipe was sent to me as a birthday present by a friend in Northampton. With my British Rail card, it consoled me for being sixty.

Dennis's Dundee Cake

1lb (450g) mixed fruit
large wine glass of sherry
6oz (175g) pitted dates
5fl oz (150ml) water
4oz (110g) margarine
3 eggs, beaten
grated rind of 1 lemon

8oz (225g) plain wholewheat
   flour
2 teaspoons baking powder
1 teaspoon mixed spice
1oz (25g) ground almonds
whole blanched almonds for
   the top of the cake

● Steep the mixed fruit in the sherry for several hours or overnight, stirring the fruit around a few times if possible.

● Put the dates and the water in a saucepan and bring to the boil, mashing the dates with a potato masher. Remove from the heat and set aside to cool.

● Mix together in a bowl with the cooked date pulp, the margarine, eggs and lemon rind. Sift in the flour, baking powder and spices (you can put in a lot more than 1 teaspoon!), adding the bran from the sifted flour at the end. Beat vigorously – 2 minutes in an electric mixer, 5 minutes if doing the job by hand.

● Stir in the mixed fruit and the ground almonds, and enough of the sherry to give a soft dropping consistency to the mixture.

● Put into a greased and lined 8-inch tin, arrange the whole almonds on the top and bake at Gas 4/350°F/180°C for about 2 hours, or until a skewer pushed into the centre of the cake comes out clean.

● Turn out, jab the top all over, then sprinkle with booze. Leave the cake for a couple of days before cutting to allow the booze to settle down.

Ma Faces the Music

My mother used to play the piano in the silent films. She knew four tunes – one for the heroine (*Hearts and Flowers*), one for the villain and one for motion (I think it was the overture to *Zampa*). The fourth was in great demand for the Keystone Cops and the fall of Babylon.

She sat on a stool underneath the flickering screen and strained her neck upwards to peer at the jerky images. It must have been very tiring, because sometimes she nearly fell asleep and banged out the wrong tune.

The tickets to Ma's fleapit cost a halfpenny or a whole penny (not 'p' but 'd'), and the clientèle expected their money's worth. They sat on wooden benches without dividers, and if the usherette piled too many on to one end, the bench acted like a seesaw, and the patrons at the other end rose involuntarily. In the darkness this could, and did, lead to a rough-house, and my mother (who was bored stiff and liked a bit of life) swiftly chucked *Hearts and Flowers*, which she despised, and urged on the combatants with *Zampa*, played with the loud pedal down.

Occasionally my mother got more embroiled than she cared to. At the cinema in those days the films may have been silent but the audience was not. They chewed, munched, sucked and masticated with intense enjoyment. Passion meant biscuits and peanuts (some of which they threw at my mother), and fish and chips and pigs' trotters. Together with an occasional whelk, they were the accompaniment to the high drama on the screen. Ice-creams and hard biscuits were well thought of, chocolate bars were regarded as sissy stuff. (I suppose that though nice enough to eat they were not very useful as weapons, unless half-melted and splodgy.)

Such cinemas died during the Second World War, but I still remember them from my childhood. Anyway, I remember eating biscuit after biscuit. They were good for gang warfare.

Here are some ginger biscuits that are delicious and almost totally healthy! So says my agent Richard Scott Simon who gave me the recipe.

Richard's Ginger Biscuits

2 tablespoons golden syrup or
  honey
3fl oz (75ml) sunflower oil
3oz (75g) plain wholemeal flour
2oz (50g) medium oatmeal
1oz (25g) pumpkin seeds,
  almonds, hazelnuts, etc.
1½oz (40g) demerara sugar

1 tablespoon crystallised or,
  better still, stem ginger,
  chopped fine
2 heaped teaspoons ground
  ginger
a pinch of salt
1 level teaspoon bicarbonate of
  soda

● Dissolve the syrup or honey in the oil – heat them gently, but do not boil.

● Mix in a bowl the flour, oatmeal, nuts (you could leave these out and make up the weight with flour and oatmeal, depending on how crunchy you like your biccies), sugar, the two kinds of ginger, salt and bicarbonate of soda. Add the syrup mixture and mix together thoroughly.

● Grease two baking trays and put on each of them teaspoonfuls of the biscuit mixture, setting these well apart and giving each mound a little press down. Bake for 25 minutes at Gas 2/300°F/150°C.

● Leave to cool for a couple of minutes, then loosen off the tray before they become too crisp and fragile. If they are not cooked enough you can return them to the oven for a few more minutes. Finish cooling the biscuits on a trivet.

The Way We Were

When I was a child, life was arranged differently. The centre of gravity of the living-room was not of course a TV set but a fireplace, and an enormous amount of activity was spent in kindling and keeping the coal fire alight. Each one of us had her or his own way of arranging the sticks and shredded paper. Some held newspaper in front of the grate, and ran for cover if it caught fire and went up the chimney, setting the soot alight. Some put bits of fat on the flames and nearly burnt the house down. It was all highly dangerous, and only paraffin was beyond the pale.

The main activity was toasting and roasting things, such as crumpets if you could get them, or chestnuts. After the War when the sweet ration made it possible, we learned from American soldiers how to toast marshmallows. I remember the wonder of watching them suddenly explode into a sticky mush.

We also stood differently, because apart from hot patches, the temperature inside a house was much the same as the temperature outside. So people took turns to stand first with their backs, then their fronts, to the fire.

There was a subsidiary centre of attention. Each house had a round Bakelite wireless in the parlour. The master of the house (it was still a sexist society) reserved for himself the role of twiddling. We all turned to it, as to an altar, for the nine o'clock news, making out the over-optimistic words through the thunder of threatening static.

There were also children's games and activities that have now fallen into disuse. Jewish children played religious games with nuts and spinning tops with Hebrew letters marked on them.

Was it a happier world? I don't know. It was certainly a simpler world, but with more prejudices, too.

We didn't buy our breakfast cereal out of packets. We made it. I'd forgotten how good home-made cereal was, until at Turvey Abbey I was given this recipe by Sister cook. I use it because oats are supposed to be good against cholesterol. Sister cook makes it 'sugarless' for a diabetic friend. Make lots and store it in the freezer.

Sister Cook's Daily Oats

6 cups oats
½ cup seasame seeds
1 cup wheat germ
1 cup oat germ
1½ cups wholewheat flour
    (granary is good)
1 cup soft brown sugar

1 teaspoon salt
½ cup hot water
¾ cup oil (sunflower if
    possible)

Sister cook uses a standard
    American cup, which is
    8fl oz.

● Mix together all the dry ingredients. Add the hot water and oil and stir well until all the oaty bits are moist.

● Spread the mixture evenly on a baking tray (preferably with 1-inch sides) and bake for 30 minutes at Gas 3/325°F/160°C.

● Take out of the oven and give the mixture a good stir, making sure the edges get mixed in. Bake for a further 30 minutes.

● Stir the mixture again and bake the oats for a third time. Sometimes only 20 minutes are needed for this last bake – the oats should be golden, dry and, after cooling a bit, quite crumbly.

● Eat with milk or yoghurt – a sliced banana on top is good.

Meditation on the New Year

I visited a fascinating exhibition for the funeral trade. The undertakers who welcomed me were caring and considerate folk, who courteously let me wander round the stalls thinking my own thoughts.

Embalming, I learned, was on the up with good prospects for a promising lad, or lass, I presume, in these days of sexual equality. I admired the stone masons' art and wondered if I could cadge a spare bit of marble for pastry-making. But on second thoughts that didn't seem seemly, so I turned to the clothing counter instead. I fancied myself in the coats with capes, sophisticated yet solemn.

But I lingered longest amongst the coffins, lined, ruched and looking rather comfortable, saying a silent prayer for an old nun I knew who used to sleep in one, though without the satin lining. In her latter days, she often used to climb into it to pause for thought.

She wasn't way out – oh, no, no, no. Lots of people like to step outside this life for a few minutes – not to deny it but to enjoy it more by getting it in perspective. If you're too caught up in this world you can't see it straight, it's too clouded by your hopes and fears. You take it too heavy and you get too worried by worldly success and failure, which come and go like the weather. That's why many contented monks and nuns 'die to the world' in special ceremonies and why many Jews complete their own New Year celebrations with a total fast, wearing their shrouds, as a foretaste of the world to come.

A public holiday is a good time to step out of life. The New Year party's over, and this is the morning after the night before. Washing-up is a meditative occupation, and the remains on people's plates are reminders of human vanity and greed. It's a bank holiday, too, so business is out, and you're inbetween two periods of time, which is good for spirituality. A mild hangover also helps your thoughts heavenwards.

So sit back, put a clean teatowel over your head, and think about what your last judgement will be like. Don't get too depressed. One teacher told me – all that will happen is that God will take you one by one to himself, put you on his knee, as it were, and show you what your life was really about. You'll see the good you did and the bad, and the difference between them will be your heaven and hell. And Rabbi

Zusya said, 'In the coming world they won't ask me why I wasn't Moses but why I wasn't Zusya.' In other words, not why you weren't superman but why you weren't yourself.

And what will heaven be like? Well, the Reverend Sidney Smith, who was C of E, said, 'It will be like eating pâté to the sound of trumpets.' So why wait? There must be some bits of pâté on those dirty plates. Find a bit without toothmarks, and consume it to some brass band music on the radio. And while you munch, remember the world we're all going to, and make your New Year Resolutions.

After funerals, Jewish people often return to the mourners' home. They expect whisky and a savoury snack. Here is one that would be acceptable.

Anchoiade

2lbs (900g) onions, finely chopped
3 tins of anchovies
salt and freshly ground black pepper
1lb (450g) packet of shortcrust pastry
chopped fresh parsley

Optional
garlic
olive oil
black olives

• Stew the onions with the anchovies and their oil, adding olive oil and garlic if you wish. Let it cook slowly to a brown, savoury, toffeeish mush.

• Add pepper but go easy on the salt.

• Roll out the pastry to pizza thickness, place on an oiled baking tray and spread the onion mixture on top. Bake in a preheated oven, Gas 4/350°F/180°C (or according to the instructions on the packet), for about 30 minutes, until the pastry is cooked.

• Scatter with chopped parsley, and black olives if you like, and cut into squares. Serve.

• If you can't be bothered with pastry, thick slices of bread will do — in which case, don't bake so long.

Pies for Scousers

I was convalescing in Tenerife, and I met a time-share tout. Wouldn't I like to retire to his high-rise apartment? I could watch the sun, day by day, bounce out of the sea at one end of my balcony and plop back in the sea at the other. I'd be bored stiff I said, and in modern developments you can often smell hamburger among the hibiscus.

'I've been thinking. We're not getting any younger, and the good Lord will soon be taking one of us, so then I'll get myself a flat in Brighton.'

NERO

Well, where was I going to retire? He might think it strange, I answered, but I was thinking of living in Liverpool. 'Very strange,' he said politely and handed me the local Spanish paper. That's how I read about the Hillsborough football tragedy. End of conversation.

So why do I prefer Liverpool? Well, it's cheap. A house there's the price of a garage in Central London. A three-course meal is three pounds, a haircut two. And you don't get bored, there's too much vitality, good nature and assertiveness.

I like looking at the girls marching to the discos at weekends – arms linked, self confident and singing. God help any lad who falls foul of them.

And in a caff, I watch an old lady munching her sarny underneath a no smoking sign, while her lower lip's glued to a fag.

And nearby, some young parents are force feeding their young with lumps of cholesterol.

And there's the DIY chap who conscientiously tries to tidy up a brick exhibit at a modern art show, to the frenzy of the attendants.

It's a moody city but the moods change fast. In a pub some youngsters, bigger than me, were going on about Jewy this and Jewy that. Before I decided to sacrifice myself, one of them, thank God, shouted, 'There's that Rabbi who cooks on the telly.' They turned round. Did I know Esther Rantzen, Terry Wogan, Derek Jameson? We chatted and they waved as they trooped out of the Chinese chippy.

Back from Tenerife I watched the memorial service on the box with friends. 'Was that another passing mood?' some asked.

'No, it's solid,' I said. 'Religion in Liverpool is real, not public relations.' I know because I'm a religious professional who can read the signs. In Liverpool churches, after the service, there's a bun for visitors and worshippers alike. But the down and outs get theirs first. I've seen it. And I've met church workers there, who care and babysit for the families they supervise.

And in the cathedral beside the pious pictures of miracles I don't quite believe in, they've put a Liverpool lady in a stained glass window who took sick prostitutes into her home. Taking your problem into your home, that's foolhardy, but religion can't get more real than that.

I get impatient with plastic people, and plastic piety, which is why Liverpool could be home. And in Liverpool I won't have to watch that silly old sun bounce up and down like a yo-yo, because most of the year there isn't any.

But I can do without the sun. Melting on a beach is not my idea of fun. I would prefer to melt cheese for a northern cheese and onion pie. Now northern pies are sensible solid affairs, which really satisfy. I can testify that this one is a good cure for hunger and depression. A slice, cold, in the middle of the night, eaten in bed, listening to BBC World Service, is an antidote to nightmares.

Tom Trow's Cheese Pie

8oz (225g) shortcrust pastry
2 large onions, chopped
1lb (450g) medium mature
  Cheddar, diced

4oz (110g) mushrooms,
  chopped small (optional)
freshly ground pepper

● Roll out the pastry and line a 7-inch (17cm) pie dish.

● Simmer the onions in a little water for 6–7 mintues and then drain.

● Melt the cheese slowly in a non-stick pan. Add the mushrooms and onions to the melted cheese in the pan and stir together. Season with a few grinds of pepper, but no salt. Pour the mixture into the pie dish.

● Bake in a preheated oven, Gas 5/375°F/190°C, for just over half an hour, until the pastry is cooked.

● It can be eaten hot or cold. Tom says 'In the north we are not mean with our cheese.'

In a Crematorium Canteen

I sit on a bench in a crematorium canteen and consider the old boy whose ashes I've just scattered, a bit of whom may be lodged in my eye. I rub it neurotically. You never know which way the wind blows.

But a little legacy has blown my way, which was nice of him. 'Spend it on what you want, not charity,' he said. But what? I've got a home and I've paid for my holiday.

Two C of E types at the next table are taking bets on the next Archbishop of Canterbury. Should I remind them that someone suggested me on the radio too! It's less impossible than Chief Rabbi.

The Walter Mitty in me starts phantasising. Looking mean and mystical, as if I'd smelt some incense that had gone off, I ascend mitred, to my archepiscopal throne, while choirs moan hosannas and acolytes do, well, whatever acolytes must do. I raise my hand hieratically and speak. But as I haven't got a clue what to say that hasn't been said by everybody before my phantasy breaks down. To cushion the shock I order a slice of chocolate cake.

As I munch it, I suddenly know what I want – a title. But as no one's going to give me one I'll have to get on my bike and buy one. An honorary doctorate in life studies, perhaps. No, I want a true blue-blooded one. If I subscribed to some order, I might become ennobled by the back door. Chevalier Bleu, I tell myself, Cavaliere Azurro, Ritter von Blau. It would sell my books in America, so it would be a legitimate business expense.

Some of the best titles in British history were bought or awarded for favours rendered, some not so respectable as my life studies.

But I remember the grave of my former girlfriend and I cringe as I hear her voice: 'Lionel Blue, how can you be so vulgar?'

Because I don't believe in myself, I suppose, only in the reflections of me in other people's minds. Through the door, I see a cortège coming out of the chapel. But if I'm made up only of reflections in other people's minds, how can any bit of me survive death? At my last judgement, there won't be any of me left to judge, if I trade in my soul for social acceptance.

I sigh. The legacy will have to go to charity, whatever the old boy said.

At the crematorium gate there are little flags with pins, exchanged for donations. I stick a large note, not a coin, into the box but fiercely refuse a flag, which puzzles the nice flag seller. No, I don't want recognition or any worldly reward. I want to save my soul. So that something of me remains, when the rest of me is also blown away by the wind.

What also remains is the memory of that chocolate cake. Here's an easy way of making that memory real.

Molly's Chocolate Cake

Here is a very simple way of turning a plain Madeira or sand cake into something utterly delicious.

● Just before you turn the plain cake mixture into its baking tin, take a quarter pound of the very best plain dark chocolate you can find and afford: Terry's, Lindt, Suchard . . . that sort of thing, but extra quality makes all the difference. Leave the chocolate in its wrapper and give it a good beating with a rolling pin. The result should be a mixture of a little dust and lots of assorted-sized chocolate pieces. Fold these into the cake mixture, and bake as usual.

● The chocolate will sink towards the bottom of the cake, but don't worry – look at the grins as the eaters hit upon the lumps of delicious chocolate.

Curious and Interesting

I am curious, not censorious, about other people's tastes. My mother used to treat herself to kippers and jam for breakfast, when most others could only manage cornflakes. A friend, who is a gourmet, surreptitiously eats pickled pig's trotters, in the darkness of cinemas, spitting out bits of bone. It was a habit he acquired in a poor hard childhood. A Mediterranean café serves rabbit in chocolate sauce to a devoted clientèle, and my grandfather liked to suck out the brains of cooked carp.

My own curiosities! I used to add so much Worcestershire sauce to tomato juice that my host suggested sarcastically that I leave out the juice – which I did. A sherry glass of Worcestershire sauce, straight, worked like a tonic. After this craving died away, another took its place. Under stress, I liked to retire to bed early with a small tin of condensed milk and a teaspoon. My two dogs approved and we were all three happy.

There is no accounting for tastes, so I shall not bother. The following recipes are all loved by someone or other, otherwise I would not have acquired them. If they are what your subconscious was secretly longing for, think how much money I've saved you in psychotherapy.

Special

Preaching to adults is easy. Teaching religion to a confirmand or a Bar Mitzvah is tough. But that's the job they usually hand out to curates and trainee inexperienced student ministers – which was me.

My classroom was a disaster area. The children shouted and threw things. I threatened and bribed them with chocolates to buy five minutes' peace. I'd no experience and they spotted it. I was also disorganised because my home life was falling to bits – which thank God they didn't spot. But they broke me down and one night before I left the synagogue I wrote out my resignation.

On the way home in the underground train I saw one of the ringleaders moodily sawing through an armrest with a penknife. I crossed the carriage. 'Stop that!' I said and couldn't help adding in self-pity, 'I'm resigning. You can make some other poor b's life a misery. You can boast about it back home.'

'Not going home,' he said sullenly.

I didn't want to either, so I stood him a sticky bun in the station caff, and heard his story. Not an abnormal one. A fragile marriage, divorce, stepmother. I didn't give him advice – only attention.

He must have appreciated it, because next lesson he punched a boy who threw a pellet at me. I took that kid out to tea too, heard him out, and some of the other mafia as well. Behaviour in class didn't become wonderful after that, but the nastiness had gone.

It could have been wonderful if I'd had the time to treat them all as special, but I didn't, I was preoccupied with my own problems. I wanted to be special too, which was a pity, because there's an extra emotional emptiness inside every hooligan who craves for special treatment. But the world has more takers than givers, so it's tough luck for them and for us.

Of course there's plenty of plastic caring around, but you can't trust it – fulsome apologies on British Rail, which sound so personal, but can't be; personalised letters printed out on word processors; universal prayers which ask too much for too many, so you don't believe in any of them.

Teachers' threats and police patrols keep the lid on the trouble-makers, but can't cure their problem. And the caring professions –

ministers, social workers and such can't care enough, because the demand is insatiable, so they begin to feel badly treated too and give up.

Like this psychotherapist who tottered to the canteen bar after his first day at the clinic. 'Give me a brandy,' he says. Then he turns to an older colleague, who is placidly consuming cream pastries. 'How can you listen to those people all day and keep so calm?' 'Who listens?' says the other, shrugging his shoulder.

Well, God listens – that's the only hope. It saved me but how do you tell that to a troublemaker in a confirmation class or a football stadium? Confirmation kids like to be treated as adults, which indeed they are, encountering passion, love, and the search for meaning in all their elemental force. 'Bandiera Italiana' – the Italian flag *hors d'oeuvre* – appealed to the adult part of them because of its taste, and the child part of them because of its looks. It is an appetising conceit.

Bandiera Italiana

2 avocados, peeled, stoned and sliced crossways
8oz (225g) Italian or Danish Mozzarella (Danish is easier on the pocket), sliced
2–3 beef tomatoes, sliced
chopped spring onions or olives
French dressing made with olive oil and lemon juice
freshly ground black pepper

● Arrange the slices of avocado, Mozzarella and tomato in alternatives stripes of the Italian flag – green, white and red. Frame with the spring onions or olives, pour over the French dressing, and season with plenty of freshly ground black pepper.

● You can use any sliceable English white cheese – after all, we're all in the EEC. I don't know how the Italians would translate our Union Jack into tablefare!

Birthday Blues

A letter plopped through the letterbox and I glanced at it, puzzled. It was from a friend who wrote asking if there'd be a celebration for the birthday. Whose birthday? Then the penny dropped – he meant mine, because in two weeks' time I'll be sixty-one.

Now sixty-one is a number you can't get excited about. At sixty I got an oldies' rail card, courtesy of BR, and while my mother rides the buses free I at least ride the rails at reduced rates. And at sixty-five the government will give me a nice solid pension book. But sixty-one is a non-event, a number you can't even divide by anything.

But time marches on, and in one direction only, as I was rudely reminded in the underground, when I politely stood up for a doddery old gent. 'Sit down, sir!' I said politely, for I was once a well brought up child. 'Sit down yer something self, Grandpa!' he spat back. You see your world grows old with you so you don't notice it.

But last week on the same line I bumped into some oldies like me on their way to Gatwick for a senior citizens romp in sunny Spain. I eyed them over my newspaper and was much cheered. The girls were lithe, lissom and blue rinsed. Their boys sported bouffant beehive hairdos over their grizzled good looks, like rising politicians or fashionable ladies in the 1950s. They were obviously going to have a ball.

Suddenly I remembered my granny. She was years younger than them when she died but I remember her as a very, very old woman, swathed in black shawls, her boots slashed to ease her bunions. And I realised that God had given me and many of my generation a second youth, a third age, whatever you want to call it, another stab at life, another chance to get it right.

And this time I might be more successful. Third-agers are released from expectation. What they've done, they've done and the rest is gravy. And they live more in the present than the future, because there isn't so much of that around. Also they joke about life, while first-agers and second-agers agonise over it.

My mother told my aunt this one, looking meaningfully at me. Three old Jewish women were making conversation.

'Oy veh!' said the first.

'Mmmm!' moaned the second.

'Oh God!' wailed the third.

'Well,' said the first briskly, 'now we've talked about the children let's have something sweet for tea.'

There's another thing that separates us third-agers from the first- and second-agers; we lived through a world war, and remember what it was like being bombed. But we were also witness to the power of the human spirit. We saw compassion grow in the shelters and in the cruelty of the concentration camps, too, and how ordinary people had strength to give their lives for others, and their last crust of bread. We know quite well the price good people pay, but we also know that evil is by its nature self-destructive, and in the end the good remains.

The ladies in the story above are obviously Jewish – gentiles do not moan that way, but they would still enjoy this Jewish version of a Christmas pudding.

'All right. So my 65-year-old husband is now running after young girls. A dog chases cars, but tell me, when he catches one, can he drive it?'

Quick Christmas Pudding

Mix together tinned, sweetened chestnut purée with an equal quantity of fromage frais. Add brandy or rum to taste (sugar too if you have a very sweet tooth). Pile into glasses, top with whipped cream, and decorate with festive bits like glacé cherries, sugared violets or rose petals, walnuts, angelica and little Father Christmases.

It's so easy!

Horrible Housework

You get curious about the people on the other side of a mike. Sometimes I try to imagine what they are like. Have they bounced out of bed, or are they still lurking under the duvet? Are they computing in an office or crashing into kippers? Perhaps they're playing their transistors in the bathroom, and splashing around with plastic ducks, which pleases more adults than people think – stockbroker types, too.

One lady wrote to me about how she feels after the nine o'clock news. 'Bloody,' she said. 'My husband's gone and so have the kids, but the washing up hasn't, and it's lurking in the sink. I've made myself a sandwich with mouldy mousetrap. Every day it's the same. Clearing up the rubbish others leave behind, knowing they'll leave the same tomorrow. I'm not a human being, just a walking dustpan. Any suggestions?' Signed 'Defeated'.

Dear defeated, yes I do have some suggestions. The first is do something with the mousetrap. Use it to wedge a door, or cook it. There's a Jewish mystical text which says, 'At the last judgement God will ask us, why didn't you enjoy all the good things in life that were permitted to you?'

So start off by filling your sandwich with something special. After all, it's your birthday. No, it isn't. Yes, it is – it's the first day of the rest of your life! What would I choose to celebrate the first day of the rest of my life? Well, my childhood delights – a chip buttie, for example. French fries inbetween two slices of cotton wool white bread, and marge, sprinkled with salt and doused with malt vinegar.

If sweetness is all, what about a Dutch treat – two slices like the last, enclosing a slice of gingerbread. A thin bar of chocolate on butter makes a nice filling too, and if you're feeling really low give it everything you've got, which means a banana and a chocolate flake mashed into condensed milk.

As to clearing up other people's rubbish, I know exactly what you mean, because that's what ministers of religion do, too – except that the dirt we clear up is inside. We try to tidy up people's sins with prayers and services, and the moment the last hymn has died away, they're all off, making their souls mucky again.

And you can also be a minister. You don't need a diploma or a dog collar, which you wouldn't want, because they're dreadful to wash unless they are plastic, which the modern ones mostly are. The greatest ministry is the ministry of the teacup. It's in a kitchen that people really pour out their souls. It's an invitation to sit in the kitchen that means real friendship. And when you're low and someone sits you down and pours you a cup of tea with a slice of cake they've made themselves, it's an unofficial communion. And a cake can provide your sermon too. If you give away a slice of cake, there's one slice less for you. But the more happiness you give away to others, the more you will have for yourself.

That's the difference between things of this world and things of the spirit. So why not invite the lonely lady down the road to join you? Make a cake, so you can have your sermon and eat it too. Then you won't feel so defeated, dear defeated!

And do something with that mousetrap. Unlike you and me it won't improve with age.

This Slaphappy Tuna Snack will use it up nicely and get you going again. Why, you might even change the washing-up water!

Slaphappy Tuna Snack

Serves 4

1 large tin of tuna	1 tablespoon chopped fresh
1 small onion, finely chopped	parsley
4–5oz (100–150g) grated	dash of anchovy essence
mousetrap	½ teaspoon paprika
1 small tin Mexicorn	1 egg
(sweetcorn with red and	4 slices bread
green pepper), drained	cayenne (optional)

● Drain the tuna and mash it. Add to it the onion, half of the mousetrap, the Mexicorn, parsley, a dash of anchovy sauce and the paprika. Bind it all with the egg.

● Toast the bread on one side, then pile the tuna mixture on the other. Sprinkle with the remaining cheese and then toast on that side too. Serve piping hot, adding cayenne if you wish.

What the Past Was Like

A TV company rang. Would I take a trip down memory lane and return to Exeter, which I left in 1940, as they wanted to make a film on the evacuation; taxi provided, and first-class train from Paddington. I would be lodged in the Royal Clarence too, no less.

I hesitated – and they thought I'd rung off. Then I said, 'Yes, delighted,' and wondered why I'd hesitated in the first place. The question niggled. Exeter's a beautiful city. Why had I avoided it in the years between? I'd driven through it, gone round it, and flown over it, but I'd never stopped in it.

Enthroned in the first class from Paddington, I brooded over the problem. The engine took me forward, and memory carried me back. In September 1939 I took the same journey, probably from the same platform – but in third class, of course, not first (second was ladies only). Soldiers, sailors and evacuees were crammed into every cranny. There was no easy-wash nylon then, so we all ponged like well-hung venison, and the smell of wet wool was everywhere. A blue bulb gleamed dimly through cigarette smoke. I cadged a fag, swallowed and was sick in the toilet.

Even as I retched, I marvelled at a train with a toilet and corridor. Till then I'd only travelled in trains with closed compartments. If you were a child and you had to spend a penny, you were lifted to the window, while your fellow travellers averted their eyes. The next carriage up was warned with thumps not to look out lest they get an eyeful. It was hell if you were a little boy, it was worse if you were a little girl.

I am recalled from 1939 to now when our train stops, and a well-bred whisper runs round the first class that there's a detour because of rail repairs. Suddenly I know why I hesitated about going back. The war years for me were a dreadful, useless detour in my life. I'd left London in 1939 a happy go lucky child. When the war ended I was a bewildered mess. In the meantime I'd been billeted on a dozen families.

And yet I was lucky. I remembered my friend Professor John Heimler, whose funeral I had just attended. He was also a happy youth, but a train took him from his home in Hungary at the same time. It carried him to a concentration camp, not to kind people in

Exeter. And yet he told me that in that hell where he lost his family he'd learnt to love human beings. Perhaps he would have learnt the same lesson elsewhere, but he didn't. In my mind my dear friend asked me, 'Did you learn anything from your wartime detour, Lionel?' I considered his question carefully. 'It can't compare with yours, John,' I answered, 'but I think so. What started off as self-pity when the war began turned into true pity for others, before the war ended. Perhaps like you I would have learnt the same lesson another way, but I didn't.'

In stations fifty years ago, a soldier in a poster looked out and asked 'Is your journey really necessary?' Are the wasted years of our life really necessary, life's detours and disappointments? With hindsight, perhaps some are. That's the only way some of us ever see the light that shines in darkness. Surely that's the religious hope.

The train slid into Exeter St Davids. It felt right to face my past. And this time I wouldn't eat Woolton Pie made with mangel-wurzels, but a cream tea in the Royal Clarence. What bliss!

But there were some wartime delights that never fade. At a sophisticated dinner party, Tom Wakefield, the novelist, and I discussed Bewildered Pilchard Pie. Later on he gave me his recipe. It's not to be despised if you want to know what life was like when there was a war on and you were the lucky one with a tin of pilchards and a lump of cheese. Tom says, 'I don't know why the pilchard is bewildered but I reckon any fish might feel a bit out of sorts if it went from ocean to can and then into an oven!'

Bewildered Pilchard Pie

Serves 2 generously

1 tin of pilchards
1lb (450g) potatoes
3–4 tablespoons milk
1 large onion, chopped
2 tablespoons oil
4oz (110g) red Leicester cheese,
    grated

salt and pepper

Posh version
above ingredients *plus*
**4oz (110g) mushrooms,
    sliced
tin of anchovies**

● Boil the potatoes and mash with the milk.

● Fry the onion in the oil until soft and add with the pilchards to the potatoes. Season with salt and pepper and mix well.

● Transfer to a casserole and sprinkle the cheese over the top. Bake in a preheated oven at Gas 4/350°F/180°C, till it's piping hot and the cheese melts and bubbles.

● To make the posh version, garnish the cheese surface with the mushroom and/or anchovies before baking. Tinned mackerel, tuna, etc., can all be substituted for pilchards if your income improves.

● Serve with a mixed salad or peas.

'Saint Wulfstan is in the Can'

We're in Worcester Cathedral making a film on English religious history. The TV crew huddle round their camera and I lean against a convenient tomb, near the remains of St Wulfstan – if they still remain, that is. A powder puff appears from nowhere and removes the shine from my nose. Surprised, I swallow my chewing gum.

'Action!' shouts the director. I step forward and speak fiercely into the camera: 'This is a holy and historic place.' Then I sneeze because the powder has got up my nose. 'Cut!' says the director, and I lean back against the tomb and wonder how real actors use their leftover time between takes. Greta Garbo thought of her next hamburger, and this gave her that yearning look in *Queen Christina.* An opera singer I know who hangs about on stage in draughty tunics mentally marks off the items on his laundry list. I try to meditate on St Wulfstan but leftover time makes me think of leftovers in my fridge. Can gravy or custard redeem them? Probably not – after all, why were they leftover in the first place? 'Action!' cries the director. 'This is a holy and historic place,' I proclaim urgently, because the cathedral tea counter is closing. This time we get it right. 'St Wulfstan is in the can.' Whoopee!

But I worry if my nose will glow on the box. I'll never know, because in the cutting room we find we've two saints too many. Wulfstan's also a leftover. 'Never *heard* of him,' you say . . . 'Never *heard* of Wulfstan, mate? Where've you been all your life?'

I only thought about him again when my leftover saint came back to life, as I was reading the papers at breakfast. Tribalism, I read, was returning to Europe. Nationalists were butchering each other in the Caucasus, and closer to home in Ireland. And German nudists had been burnt out of their holiday camp by Corsican patriots.

There were the same national passions in Wulfstan's time, for he was the Saxon bishop when William the Conqueror reduced the Saxons to serfdom. To save everyone from civil war, Wulfstan didn't try to cut the King down. He co-operated with him instead and they stopped the cruel trade in Saxon slaves from Bristol. He knew you mustn't try to love your own people more by loving other people less, for God isn't your tribal totem but God of your enemies, too, a lesson which Europe with all its theology and cathedrals still hasn't learnt.

So, come back, St Wulfstan, we daren't leave you out. Kneecapped Irishmen, mourning Caucasians and nudist Germans need you now.

While filming, I used to discuss food with Jan and Krystyna Kaplan, the celebrated producer and director. Krystyna comes from north-east Poland, not far from my own family three or four generations back. Just reading this recipe takes me back to my childhood in my grandparents' kitchen. True Slav cuisine is an acquired taste, but once you've acquired it any other cuisine, apart perhaps from Indian, seems anaemic somehow.

Cucumber Soup (made out of cucumbers in brine)

1 medium tin of cucumbers in brine

3 pints (1.8 litres) stock, made from root vegetables (carrots, parsnips, onion, celery, leek), peppercorns, 1–2 bay leaves, bouquet garni, pimento (optional); chicken wings (free range or kosher) can also enrich this stock

4 potatoes
½ pint (10fl oz) milk
2 tablespoons flour
2–4 tablespoons unsalted butter
1 egg yolk
salt and pepper
chopped fresh parsley

Krystyna writes:

● This is the most delicious Polish soup. Prepare a good stock of vegetables, with chicken if you like. Once or twice I have used *dashi* (a Japanese stock made out of dried bonito) but orthodox Polish cooks could be quite shocked by my uninhibited combinations . . . When the stock is ready, strain it and throw a few potatoes in, and boil until soft.

● Meanwhile, grate the cucumbers, bought in a tin or a jar or from a barrel, on a grater with large holes. Put it aside and reserve the brine from the tin.

● When the potatoes are ready, add to the stock the cold milk mixed with the flour. Boil it briefly.

- Rub the butter with the egg yolk into a paste and dilute it with some of the soup and then pour it back into the pot. Switch off the heat.

- Add the grated cucumbers and the brine, salt and pepper, sprinkle it with parsley and serve.

- The soup will have a delicate soury-salty taste with a sweetness of a good stock underneath. Add as little or as much brine you like, according to your taste.

Burnt Offerings

Now is the time for sitting in my garden. Last year, a friend built a patio on it, and, greatly daring, I went out and bought a mini barbecue from the supermarket for the real Texas touch.

But do I dare use it? I usually plead pseudo-sickness whenever invited to a barbecue party. 'Smoke gets in your eyes', as the lovely old song says, and sometimes a chip off the old charcoal too, and I can't consume and make conversation with only one eye and that rimmed with red.

You need both eyes at a barbecue. Though you can tell by touch which side your bread is buttered, you can't tell without looking which side of your chop is burnt and which is bloody. Nothing can ever be cooked through, though the whiff of methylated on the meat suggests the cook has tried to help on his charcoal. I do not recommend it.

Instead of the traditional bottle of plonk, bring medical plasters with anti-burn dressing instead. Your offering will not be thought well of at first, but as little screams and squeals come from the cooks, your reputation will rise like the flames.

At barbecues you will be expected to be tough as well as Texan – which means no knives and forks but fingers – so bring along some kitchen tongs to help you consume sausages without weals. Also, any instrument that can work out which way the breeze blows so you can stand upwind of it.

I've often wondered what sacrifices in the ancient world were like. Were they like barbecues? I know they were holy, but were they hygienic? Broiled sausages and chops can cause a conflagration with the best modern equipment. What could it have caused with a whole heifer, ox or sheep? How right the prophets were when they said the sacrifice of the Lord's was 'a broken and contrite heart'. Much more spiritual, and much less messy.

If, after all this, you are still determined to broil, burn, and smoke yourself as well as your food, then try these peppers which are red without being bloody, and charring actually improves them.

Barbecued Red Peppers

red peppers   salt and freshly ground
oil (use the best olive)   pepper

● Wash the whole peppers and rub them lightly with olive oil.

● Barbecue them until the flesh is soft, and the skins are charred. Use long tongs, not hands, to turn them. If you wish, crumble off the scorched skins (in a brown paper bag), though some people like the scorched bits. But you must cut them in two, and discard all the seeds and innards.

● Dribble a little more oil over them, and sprinkle with a little salt and pepper. They will be quite hot to handle, so you may need gloves. Serve.

Convenience Coleslaw

● For a side salad all you need is a really big bowl of coleslaw. Thinly slice ½ red cabbage, ½ white cabbage, 1 Spanish onion, 1 green pepper. (A food processor with a slicing attachment is perfect for the job.) Add 3 or 4 grated carrots, a handful of raisins, and chopped cashew nuts if you have a packet.

Use an adventurous dressing. I won't waste my time being subtle at barbecues. Buy a bottle of thousand island or blue cheese dressing. Corn relish is good with corn cobs too.

Wardwise

In the last year, I've had long stretches in hospital and become very wardwise, and these are my basics for ward survival.

Learn your number by heart, and recite it regularly every morning after prayers like Amen. If your file gets lost, or you fall into a black hole of the hospital computer, the ritual recitation of your number can work like an incantation. It can stop you becoming a non-person, the object of pity or accusation, a lodger in limbo.

Communal sleeping is possible, provided you come prepared with the equipment you would take to a boisterous hotel on a costa. Ear plugs for the snores and sun lamp goggles for the lights! I speak of men's wards. Whether women snore is unresolved. It requires research.

Since your innards are messy, let your outards be bright. Sunshine yellow, puce, bright blue, and fire engine red will brighten you up and the ward. Instead of pyjamas, try beach suits, holiday shirts, sarongs over Y-fronts, and jogging pants. They give some dash to a desperate situation.

If you bring a radio, bring personal earphones. Hopefully you will have to live alongside your neighbours for some time, and they may not share your taste for sackbuts on Radio Three.

Take the books you really enjoy, not the ones you think you ought to enjoy. Personally, I read unintellectual detective stories, with no blood, because there is too much of the real stuff around.

Inform friends and family that a ward is not a hot-house in Kew Gardens, so posies, please, not wreaths or pots no patient has the strength to irrigate.

I can't tell you about ward recipes, because there are few facilities for gastronomic expertise in a ward. But I can tell you about the one luxury I longed for – a smoked salmon sandwich. I call this . . .

Perfection

You will need: two slices of thin white bread, decrusted, and really fresh, unsalted creamery butter; two generous slices of Scotch smoked salmon, each enough to cover the bread; half a teaspoon of the most finely chopped raw onion you can manage without mincing your fingertips; a small sprinkle of freshly squeezed lemon juice; a few grains of cayenne pepper.

Assemble the sandwich in the following order: bread, butter, salmon, onion, lemon juice, cayenne, salmon, butter, bread. There is a Jewish variant, equally good. Split a fresh beigel instead of two slices of bread, and substitute thick full fat cream cheese for butter. Proceed as above.

Close the curtains round your bed because it excites envy, but this cannot be shared. That's life and life's tough as the wardwise can tell you.

Ordinary!

A lady asked me why I was so interested in saints and shrines. Professionally, I told her, because I too was a holy man once. It was the result of no nicotine. I'd been a heavy smoker, and when I stopped my body chemistry collapsed. My juices gurgled, my gases grunted or, worse, my eyes couldn't focus and my mind wouldn't. But some religious romantics called my new loony look mystic, and I began to believe it. My saintly status didn't last, because whenever I smelt cigarettes I snarled and snapped, which holy men don't do. As my disciples only wanted a human prayer wheel to keep the command-ments that they didn't, we deserved each other.

But I did become curious about real holy people. They weren't rare and romantic as I'd thought, but rather ordinary. I even discovered one among my acquaintances at an interfaith conference in Germany.

I was puzzled by a glum Turk who sat in the back row, not understanding a word. Was he interested in Christians? 'Not much,' translated the interpreter. 'Jews, then?' 'Not at all.' So why was he here? The Turk pointed to a pastor I knew. 'Because of him, he is holy.' My pastor was the only one who had welcomed him into a cold Western city as a human being and a brother.

'Do you know any saints?' I asked my pastor curiously. 'Yes,' he said. 'A Russian prisoner in 1943 who nursed wounded German soldiers, like his own family.' 'Are you like him?' 'Don't be silly, I told you he was a saint!'

St Walston, whose shrine I visited, was ordinary and extraordinary like that. An upper class Saxon who, like the Irish monks, decided to go wherever God sent him, even to the ends of the earth. Well, his cart got stuck in a farmyard, only a few miles away, and the animals wouldn't budge. The farmer needed a labourer, so that's what Walston became and remained for the rest of his life – an ordinary Norfolk farm labourer who healed animals and humans. There's the usual fuzz of miracles, but that glitz doesn't count.

What does is his message in that shrine. *Where* you are may be where God wants you to be. Even ordinary washing-up can be your way to heaven, if you do it with devotion. Yes, even with a washing-up machine. So get on with it, girls and boys. Cut through that grease.

You'll love it, like the saint says. Though a glass of cooking sherry helps. Are you holy at your work?

This recipe – make no pretence about it – is hard work, as Krystyna Kaplan says. But hard work never hurt anybody, and why not use a processor? Anyway, here is her recipe for 'Grapeshots'.

Potato Meat Balls or in the Eastern part of Poland we call them 'Grapeshots'

6lb (2.7kg) large potatoes
1lb (450g) minced meat
2 onions
1 tablespoon oil

1 dry bread roll, soaked in
   water until soft
beef stock cube
salt and freshly ground pepper

• Boil one third of the potatoes in their skins until soft. Peel them and put them through a mincer. Grate the remaining two thirds of raw potatoes, using the side of the grater with the small holes, and rinse in a strong cotton or linen (absolutely clean) kitchen towel until your hands ache and the grated potato looks 'dry'. Mix together both potato doughs (the boiled and minced with the raw and grated).

• Fry the onions in the oil until golden brown and sweet. Add the meat and fry till the redness goes. Gently squeeze the water out of the bread roll, then crumble it in with the meat. Crumble the beef stock cube into it and add salt and pepper.

• Form 'mango' size dumplings of the potato dough, and stuff with the meat mixture. Gently lower the dumplings into boiling salted water and simmer until cooked.

• Serve sprinkled with chopped and fried onion.

• Krystyna says: 'Store the leftover dumplings in the fridge and the next day slice and fry them. By then, the dumplings will have a dark grey colour which would look very elegant on a Volvo but not on a plate, at least that's what Jan says. However, to me the colour is part of that wonderful taste of boiled, grated, re-boiled and fried potatoes.'

Rabbi Blue says, 'Bon appétit, and the best of British luck!'

A Lesson in RI

It's too hot to go away so I sit in the attic sorting out jumble for charity. I inspect some shoes my dog chewed, and a dusty old prayer book. But I spot my father's initials and put it aside. I also put aside a limp leather copy of Donne's love poems, inscribed by a girl called Salmon. What were her parents thinking of? But perhaps it was my pet name for her. I was always partial to salmon, especially smoked.

I untie a bundle of school reports. Religious Instruction obviously wasn't my line. 'Absences,' I read! 'No application.' Yet en route I did pick up some religion. I remember two lessons.

One, in Infant School which I attended at the age of five. We were given orange plaques with pictures, to match against posters on the wall. A little girl dropped hers, and I picked it up for her. Miss Bowyer, for that was our teacher's name, told the class what a nice little boy I was, and I could sit beside her. My cup ran over. Years later I read some lines of the Roman emperor Marcus Aurelius: 'I have seen the nature of goodness, and know that it is beautiful.' Well I saw it at the age of five, and it looked like Miss Bowyer.

I also remember one RI period. Being an awkward child, I was an easy Aunt Sally for any teacher. After a frightful lesson the teacher told me to stay behind. But why, because he didn't go for me again. Then the penny dropped. He was trying to say sorry. I was so surprised, I bolted. But I learned repentance and the forgiveness of sin.

My mother peeps into the attic. 'Not much for charity,' she remarks. She's right. I can't let things go. Now why didn't they teach me useful religion in RI, like how to let go, not just of things, but of people you love who don't love you, and life itself when your time's up. Or how to listen with your whole heart, or be honest to yourself and God, or hold fast to your own truth. Instead we were taught where the Red Sea was!

But the dog-chewed shoes remind me of a student who said, 'I don't learn religion from my rabbi, I just watch how he ties his shoelaces.' Religion isn't what you teach but the way you teach it. You're your own living textbook.

I sigh and add Donne's poems to the charity pile. I'm too old for such naughtiness anyway. Also my father's prayer book, for though no scholar he was a generous man. And with two diplomas in divinity I can't do less, so I fork out a fiver from my pocket.

I award myself B— — for religion, a pass but only just.

At school, during the war, we ate a slab of bread and jam for lunch. The worst jam I ever tasted was wartime marrow and ginger. The best is the following. It's worth the effort.

Wild Apricot Jam

Makes about 5lb (2.25kg)

8oz (225g) best dried apricots	2 lemons
8oz (225g) wild hunza apricots	3lb (1.35kg) cane sugar or
3 pints (1.7 litres) water	preserving sugar

● Chop the dried apricots and soak overnight in 1½ pints (845ml) of the water. In another basin soak the whole hunza apricots in the rest of the water for the same amount of time.

● When soaked, remove the stones from the hunza apricots, chop the flesh and add with the soaking water to the first lot of apricots and water.

● Crack the apricot kernels (messy) and pour boiling water over the emerging nuts to remove their skins.

● Simmer the fruit in a preserving pan until soft – about 30 minutes – then add the juice of the lemons, the nuts and the sugar.

● Let the sugar dissolve slowly, then boil at fever pitch until the setting point is reached.

● Pour into sterilised pots and seal.

● It does not set hard; more like a conserve. This is not only good on bread and toast but also in puddings, inside sponge cakes and, perhaps best of all, Bulgarian style – by the spoonful, neat.

Honesty

Here's some gratuitous advice on marriage, a state of affairs I've never experienced and at sixty not likely to try. Yes, yes, I've got a nerve, but I do know quite a lot about it in reverse, because for eighteen years I dealt with religious divorce for the Reformed Jewish communities in this country.

Some mysteries never become clear. When I asked quarrelling couples why they got married in the first place, most could only say, 'Rabbi, it seemed a good idea at the time.'

But it did become clear that though short relationships can work for a while on phantasy, long-term ones never do. They need honesty. So when I marry couples now, for their sakes I don't avoid the inconvenient question. 'Do you both mean the same thing by the ceremony?' It's better to face it before with love than after with recrimination.

And though I feel a spoilsport, I tell them they won't stay the same. They'll change, and so will their needs, but if they can be honest about them with each other, they'll be able to renew their marriage, for within a good marriage, you divorce and remarry many times.

The advice is the same for religious relationships. People complain that God has died on them. Often it's because they've grown up, but their religion hasn't been allowed to, and holiness without honesty isn't on.

In my life I've gone through many Gods, all within the same religion. There was the God who would save me from Hitler if I didn't walk on the cracks between paving stones. There was the God who would set the universe off-course to suit my convenience. There was the God of my own group, partial and therefore dangerous.

God helped me to make them, God helped me to break them. If I hadn't, my religion would be as fragile as the marriages in my files.

That's why I sit in an empty synagogue trying to relate my religion to reality, as the Jewish New Year begins. It's time to renew my faith, for neither it nor I stood still in the past year. I can't give you the traditional apple dipped in honey, the sign of a sweet year. So instead I'll give you this New Year story about them to warn you against shameful cover-ups, and a simple sweet ecumenical recipe instead.

Some congregants spotted their rabbi in a most unsuitable, opulent restaurant, just before the New Year.

'Rabbi, what are you doing here?'

'I'm only here for the art,' he said hurriedly. 'Look at the beautiful ceiling and the decorations and oil paintings.'

Suddenly, to his horror, the waiters brought in a boar's head on a silver salver. The rabbi gulped, grabbed a pot of honey and said, 'Just look with what style they serve the apple.'

Tch—tch—tch—tch.

May the future be sweet and honest for you!

And here is my sweet ecumenical suggestion. At Buckfast Abbey, the Abbot gave me some bottles of Buckfast Tonic Wine. I told him it would be nice on vanilla ice cream. He said to take the lids off hot mince tarts, pour a generous tot in each and cover with the lids and cream, which is very good ecclesiastical advice.

'My husband has been missing for nearly a week. He's about five feet tall, bandy-legged, bald, cross-eyed, walks with a limp, has a large stomach and stutters badly. On second thoughts, don't bother.'

Postscript

If you are awake at night worrying because you can't get to sleep, remember there is no divine command about it. Relax, read a recipe, smile over a Jewish joke, ponder a spiritual story. Don't count sheep, just the things that you can be thankful for – the illnesses you never got, the things you did well, the fact that you've survived so far in a tricksy world. Watch the moonlight tumbling through the window, and think of the people who are awake like you – you're not alone – truck drivers, cleaners, nurses, nightclub dancers and nuns. You're in interesting company. Why not say a small prayer for them, it won't hurt.

And for yourself, invite the angels of your childhood into your room for company. Michael, Gabriel, Raphael and most welcome of all your guardian angel. Hold his hand, so to speak, but don't speak and . . .

Index

All-in-a-plate soup, 47
Anchoiade, 160
Anglo-Chinese soup, 59

Banana bread, 149
Bandiera Italiana, 169
Barbecued red peppers, 181
Bewildered pilchard pie, 176
Boodle's orange fool, 125
Brown bread ice cream, 135
Buckfast Abbey mince tarts, 189
Businesspeople's chicken, 85

Cabbage noodles, 101
Carbonade, 91
Cauliflower salad, 113
Chocolate cake, 151
Comforting red cabbage, 99
Convenience coleslaw, 181
Cornish pasties, 87
Crunchy, creamy apple pudding, 121
Cucumber soup, 178
Cullen skink, 56

Dennis's Dundee cake, 154
Desperation beans, 109

Edith's South American cuca cake, 147
Exotic burghul salad, 111
Exotic fish fingers, 72
Exotic sandwiches, 31

Father Robert's bobotie, 96
Fish pie, 63
Frisian hunters' dish, 115

Georgina's lentil soup, 51
Granny's baked fish, 70
Granny's salmon fish cakes, 65
Green minty melon, 20

Herrings in cream, 33
Honey meat loaf, 89

Jewish-gentile penicillin – Kim's chicken soup, 54
June's quick syllabub, 138

Kim Holman's fish cakes, 80

Lemon kippers, 22

Molly's chocolate cake, 165
Mrs Carey's confections, 140
Mushrooms in cider vinegar, 24

Omelette Hilda Lessways, 67
Onion soup, 41

Party consommé, 43
Party pie, 117
Pasta with cauliflower sauce, 78
Pauline's quick tomato soup, 49
Pennies from heaven, 107
Perfection, 183
Polish beef olives, 94
Potato meatballs, 185

Quick Christmas pudding, 171
Quick lemon pud, 133

Rich mushroom soup, 39
Richard's daily bread, 145
Richard's ginger biscuits, 156

Simple celery and lentil soup, 45
Simple savoury lentils, 103
Sister Ann's Irish soda bread, 143
Sister cook's daily oats, 158
Sister Lucy's haddock au gratin, 76
Sister Mary Camilleri's swift sweet, 131
Slaphappy tuna snack, 173
Sort of salad Niçoise, 105
Spiced Cox's apples, 127
Spreading on beigels, 26

Stuffed pitta, 29
Stuffed sardines, 35

Taramasalata, 17
Tarte des demoiselles Tatin, 129

Theo's casserole, 83
Tom Trow's cheese pie, 163
Trout royale, 74

Wild apricot jam, 187